GARY PLAYER'S
BLACK BOOK

GARY PLAYER'S BLACK BOOK

WITH MICHAEL VLISMAS

60 TIPS ON GOLF, BUSINESS, AND LIFE FROM THE BLACK KNIGHT

FOREWORD BY LEE TREVINO

Skyhorse Publishing

Skyhorse Publishing books may be purchased in bulk at special discounts for sales promotion, corporate gifts, fund-raising, or educational purposes. Special editions can also be created to specifications. For details, contact the Special Sales Department, Skyhorse Publishing, 307 West 36th Street, 11th Floor, New York, NY 10018 or info@skyhorsepublishing.com.

Skyhorse® and Skyhorse Publishing® are registered trademarks of Skyhorse Publishing, Inc.®, a Delaware corporation.

Visit our website at www.skyhorsepublishing.com.

10 9 8 7 6 5 4 3 2 1

Library of Congress Cataloging-in-Publication Data is available on file.

Interior images courtesy of Black Knight Archives

Cover photo credit Black Knight Archives

ISBN: 978-1-5107-1680-3
Ebook ISBN: 978-1-5107-1681-0

Printed in China

CONTENTS

FOREWORD

A person like Gary Player does not come around very often. His tireless and selfless way of giving back to the world, especially to the disadvantaged, has been honored for decades and will no doubt be remembered by generations.

I am fortunate enough to call Gary a friend and, on many occasions, have been a firsthand witness to his altruism. Whether yelling across the golf range to a young boy to help him with his technique or stopping to chat with an old fan while he is in the middle of a round, Gary can connect with people from all walks of life.

Hence, I was honored when Gary asked me to write a foreword for his *Little Black Book: 60 Tips on Golf, Business, and Life from the Black Knight.*

He has dined with royalty, but also with the poorest of the poor in third-world countries. He brought himself, and his family, out of near poverty. Gary often talks about how he suffered like a junkyard dog, and how it made him face adversity head-on.

If ever there were a man people should take advice from, it's Gary. And that is what you will find in this book—straightforward solutions garnered from a lifetime travelling the world that can help people of all ages and all walks of life. Enjoy.

—Lee Trevino

INTRODUCTION

"What do I do?"

Every one of us asks this question on a daily basis.

It doesn't matter whether we're trying to negotiate our way through the minefield that parenthood can be, or on the golf course with a one-shot lead playing a difficult par-four closing hole, or sitting in the office mulling over a big business decision, we all get to the point where we ask this question: "What do I do?"

I remember very well asking this question at a critical time early in my life.

I was 17 years old. I had finished high school at King Edward VII in Johannesburg. My love for golf was growing, and I believed I knew what the next step in my life would be.

"I'm going to turn professional," I told my father. He was shocked by my decision.

While my mother was suffering from cancer and shortly before she passed away when I was eight years old, she had made my father promise that I would go to university after school.

And now here I was flipping the script.

My father was devastated, and no doubt he was asking the same question of "What do I do?" in terms of how best to advise and support me as his son, but while feeling like he was also not betraying his wife's dying wish.

Having witnessed my father's reaction, I also began to question the decision that had seemed so certain to me when it first crossed my mind. "What do I do?" I began to ask myself. Do I follow my passion? If I do, it could end up making my father very sad. Or do I ignore my passion and go to university?

"What do I do?"

I'm 81 years old now, and often I still think back to that 17-year-old boy and wonder how on earth he was able to make that decision.

I don't have a foolproof way for making such decisions. But I like to think I have something far better than a magic recipe for decision making. I have a life of good experience. I have a vault of decisions—good and bad—that I have made over the years, and I can learn from these, as I still do to this day.

When it comes to my golf, I have always maintained, "The harder I practice, the luckier I get." Well, I believe the same when it comes to making decisions. The more decisions I make, the better I become at making decisions.

I've learned over time that you can't just expect yourself to make great decisions. In my case, I believe it's more a collection of things that need to come together for me to make a good decision.

It takes life experience, and the wisdom this brings. But then you also need to be careful about this, because the wisdom of your life is not necessarily the wisdom of somebody else's life.

Plus, in order to eventually figure out how to make the right decisions, you need to get a few wrong. It's what we mean when we refer to "learning from our mistakes."

From a golfer's perspective, it's like hitting balls on the range. A golfer heads to the driving range not to hit perfect shots. On the contrary, he or she heads to the range to work on the bad shots. And you've got to hit some bad shots to know what you need to work on.

Ultimately, you begin to develop what people often call that little voice in their heads, which takes into account past experiences and uses them to advise you going forward.

Over the years I became better at hearing this voice and made my decisions accordingly. They weren't always easy decisions to make, and many people thought they were the wrong decisions, but I knew that if I listened to that voice they would be the right decisions for me.

Even recently I had to listen very carefully to that voice when a number of other voices were suggesting otherwise.

I was one of those who campaigned for golf to be readmitted to the Olympic Games, and it was a proud moment when this became a reality.

I thought our game's leading professionals would embrace this opportunity—an opportunity that was denied so many of us for generations.

I would've given anything to play for South Africa in an Olympics and to add a gold medal to my career. Though South Africa was excluded from Olympic participation from 1964 to 1988 because of apartheid, I always followed the Olympics with great interest. I remember attending the 1956 Olympics and meeting Jesse Owens, and it was an incredible moment for me. I have always been fascinated by this gathering of the world's greatest athletes on one stage.

Yet in the 2016 Summer Olympics, we saw the withdrawals of golf's biggest names worldwide.

One of the main arguments from the players who were withdrawing was the supposed threat posed by the Zika virus.

I'm sorry. While I remain respectful of the personal opinions regarding this virus, it just wasn't a good enough excuse for me. I travelled for 64 years to countries with malaria, polio, typhoid, and yellow fever.

There were some complaints about scheduling, as well. Granted, this was a packed golf year and I don't think we'll have the same scheduling issues at the next Olympics.

But I felt there wasn't enough of an understanding from the players who were withdrawing that golf's return to the Olympics for the first time in over a century will naturally come with a few logistical issues at first. Yet I'm confident the officials will have sorted out these issues at the next Olympics in Tokyo in 2020.

There were other concerns as well, including security issues in Rio.

So the question remained, "What do I do?" regarding my own opinion to vote for or against the inclusion of golf at the 2016 Games, and then as to whether to attend the Games while so many were withdrawing. Golf was split down the middle in terms of the opinions for and against our inclusion into the Olympic Games.

And that's when I remembered the very first Million Dollar Golf Challenge we had at Sun City in South Africa.

It was in 1981, shortly after I had finished designing and building the Gary Player Country Club course.

My idea, heavily supported by my good friend Lee Trevino, was that the best way to market this resort would be to host the first golf tournament offering a million-dollar first prize.

Sol Kerzner, the South African hotel magnate and developer of Sun City, agreed to my concept on one condition—we had to get the top players.

I personally asked some of the world's best players to come, one of them being my good friend Jack Nicklaus.

Bear in mind the kind of global star Nicklaus was (and still is, in my mind), and then factor in that South Africa was at the time an international pariah because of the country's apartheid policy.

We had been banned from all major sporting competition. International teams and sportsmen were similarly discouraged from competing in South Africa. But there were split opinions on this. Our great leader Nelson Mandela always spoke of the power of sport to unite our people, and back in 1981 there were many—including myself—who believed crossing racial and cultural barriers in our sport would be the start of eventually doing so in our politics, as well.

But not everybody saw it this way, and there was tremendous pressure on Jack not to come and play. I know he received a personal letter from the tennis legend Arthur Ashe pleading with him not to play in that first Million Dollar Golf Challenge.

Jack was between a rock and a hard place, and I know it was a very difficult decision for him to make.

When he decided to come and play, it was because he thought that through his golf—and sport in general—he could maybe play a part in a positive solution and affect change for the good.

That's the thought that came into my mind as I wrestled with my own decision as to whether I should fully support the Olympic golf cause or not.

Once I had made that decision, the rest was easy.

I immersed myself in the Olympic spirit. I was at our country's Olympic send-off in Johannesburg, and then flew to Rio.

From Johannesburg we travelled to São Paulo, where I made my connecting flight by a mere few minutes. In my rush, my suitcase with all my Olympic clothing was left behind, but my support team managed to secure it for me.

We landed in Rio and travelled to the Olympic Village, driving past the Gavea Golf Course, where I shot a 59 in winning the 1974 Brazilian Open.

We arrived at the Village at around 11 p.m. I was completely knackered and just fell into my bed, which resembled an old army cot. On Friday morning I woke up with a stiff hip, which Avi, our physio, sorted out in no time. And then I made my way to breakfast and mingled with the athletes of the world.

My wife Vivienne also travelled to Rio and stayed in a hotel, but I was determined to experience everything of the Olympics, including life in the Village.

And then came the moment of the Games for me—the Opening Ceremony.

To walk into the Maracanã Stadium third out of the more than 200 countries present sent shivers down my spine.

I had not felt this proud being a South African for many years. Personally, being named captain of the South African Olympic golf teams was one of the great honors of my life.

As a golfer I had never walked into an arena with nearly 80,000 people cheering wildly.

I made it back to bed at 2 a.m.—dead tired, but inspired.

That experience alone had already made everything worthwhile for me, no matter what happened in the golf competitions to come.

I think this is what those golfers who decided to pass up this opportunity will regret the most—being part of something bigger.

That is another key ingredient in making decisions that I have tried to use, namely, looking beyond just yourself and seeing the bigger picture.

Making successful decisions is not just about making popular decisions or selfish decisions, it's also about making decisions with the bigger picture in mind.

And there was definitely a bigger picture involved here.

After very little sleep following the Opening Ceremony, I decided it would be best to get a good workout in the gym in the Olympic Village. I have been an athlete my entire life, and the opportunity to mix and work out with athletes at the peak of their powers from around the world was something I wasn't going to pass up.

Later that day I was invited to join the South African Sevens Rugby team for lunch and a talk about sport and life and in general. I had the opportunity to share some of my experiences with other sportsmen, and I was honored to be able to do so.

It was a busy time in the days thereafter, which included a Laureus Academy breakfast and countless media interviews. There was also my official duty as captain of the South African Olympic golf teams.

In between my official duties I found time to take Vivienne to the Sevens Rugby finals. She is a great rugby fan, and we both thoroughly enjoyed the carnival atmosphere of Sevens Rugby. That time we had together, just the two of us watching an Olympic competition live, was so special. For too long in our lives Vivienne was simply a spectator watching me compete, and now here we were—two old folks still madly in love—watching a match together and cheering wildly for South Africa.

Looking back now at the great finish we had to the men's golf competition, with Justin Rose edging Henrik Stenson for gold, and the women's event, seeing the extremely talented Inbee Park taking gold over the equally impressive Lydia Ko, I have no doubt as to the success of golf's return to the Olympic Games.

The final hour of the men's golf competition had the second highest television viewership in North America of a final round in golf this year, and behind only The Masters.

At the close of the women's competition, I remember sitting in my room that night and feeling a tremendous sense of elation, pride, and amazement at that which I'd been privileged to be part of.

Golf has been the anchor and provider for my family for 64 years. It has given me so much in life, and here it was giving me still more.

I was pleased that I had made the decision I did.

Listening to that voice inside me allowed me to make new friends and share in the great experience of the gathering of the world's finest athletes.

For maybe just a short period of time sport had allowed us all to forget about the world's problems and to embrace one another with love and respect.

And you know what? I never saw a single mosquito.

This was my Olympic decision, and I know I made the right choice in the face of so much conflicting advice and opinions.

You too are faced with your own questions and situations about which you need to make daily decisions.

On a golf course, you usually have a caddie to help you answer that question of "What do I do?"

But in life and business it's often a different story.

Many times you have people and circumstances pulling you in all sorts of different directions, and influencing your decision-making process.

Sometimes you need that "caddie" there who will give you a straight-up-and-down answer. No frills and fancies. Just an honest opinion based on experience.

Well, I hope this book can do that for you.

In all my travels around the world, meeting everybody from royalty to presidents to billionaires to ordinary parents and young people, I've looked at some of the most common questions I always get asked.

"What do I do?" in this life situation.

"What do I do?" in this golf situation.

"What do I do?" in this business situation.

If you've ever wanted to know "What would Gary Player do?" then here it is—my Black Book of some of the most common questions I've been asked throughout my life.

And this is what I would do.

A word of advice, though. This is what *I* would do. But you are not me. I have made good decisions and bad decisions. I get things right, and I get a lot of things wrong.

But to use the metaphor of golf, I've played a few courses in my time, and I can at least tell you how the ball will bounce on them.

So please don't see this as a definitive guide or answer to the questions you are grappling with.

I'd be far happier if you would simply use this book as another way that helps you hear your own small voice a little better.

And hopefully this helps you to become a better person, as well.

PART I

THE QUESTIONS OF LIFE

One of the golden rules for a caddie is to never point out the negatives to the golfer.

Telling a golfer, "Just don't hit it in the water" is going to make for a short career as a caddie.

So instead of starting off with what we don't know when it comes to life, which is a lot, let's start off with what we do know.

Life is all about challenging yourself.

The sooner you wrap your head around this, the better your decision-making process will be.

In life you are guaranteed your fair share of adversity and tough decisions, and accepting that challenge—or even embracing it—helps you succeed in the long run. In many ways, it is a lot like Major championship golf.

The Majors aren't easy, and that's because they aren't meant to be. If they were, we'd all be winning Majors like club championships.

The Majors can make you rage with frustration or break down in tears. A US Open can make you do both just on the front nine.

I always accepted that the Majors were going to be tough, and I prepared myself for that challenge. When things got tough, I was expecting it and so could deal with it far better than somebody who had a different expectation and then saw this experience as "unfair."

So to start with, recognize the decision you are facing as a chance for growth and deeper understanding of just how much you are capable of when placed under pressure. Then you'll make strong decisions. It's when you try and find the easy way out or try and make a decision based on avoiding the tough consequences thereof that you make poor decisions.

My father taught me a very valuable lesson in terms of what it means to make solid decisions about your life, starting with deciding to approach life positively.

Despite the sadness in my father's life of losing his wife to cancer, and despite the hard physical work he endured doing a very unglamorous job working in a mine for hours on end, he was still a fulfilled man. He laughed loudly. He really connected with people, and people loved him.

In a way, he defined a different kind of success for me. He made me realize that success is also an outlook rather than your environment. You can be beset with challenges in your life, but if you are determined to approach it with a positive attitude, then that in itself is a major success.

We are so frightened of failure, or of making the wrong decision. But we are guaranteed to fail in life. Our aim is not to go through life without making a single mistake. It's to live life better despite our mistakes.

And a wrong decision is wrong by whose standards? I know when I started to get into the horse business, some people thought I was mad. Then again, just because I may think stamp collecting is a mad hobby doesn't make it a wrong decision for my neighbor to go out and start collecting stamps, now does it?

Through the tough decisions my father had to make for three children he had to raise on his own, I learned so much about making decisions. I learned by simply watching how a humble man took on a very difficult life with a quiet determination to do his best for his family.

I've always tried to do the same with mine. Of course it hasn't been easy.

I've got six children and 22 grandchildren. I joke that I need to keep playing tournaments just to break even.

As much as we have been blessed as a family, it has also been a life of many tears because there were so many good-byes.

We had to make some tough decisions as a family. Vivienne would often suffer the wrath of some teachers as she took the children out of school—a lot. But she was always adamant that they must see their father.

That led to quite a different life for the children. It was a privileged life, no doubt about it, and as parents we faced tough decisions on how to keep our children grounded in the very transient world of international flights and hotels.

I remember we came back from one trip, and our son Marc had to write about it for his school. He was about 9 years old at the time. He wrote the entire essay about what he ate for breakfast, lunch, and dinner and the fact that he ordered from room service.

And I faced the constant decision of having to take myself away from my family to be able to best provide for them and realize my own dreams. The result was that I missed out on a lot. I was never there for school plays, parent meetings, sports, or anything like that. Vivienne went by herself. Golf was first in my life, and it was hard on us as a family.

The decision I made to pursue a life as a professional golfer has been a wonderful blessing to us as a family. But it doesn't mean that my decision has made me immune to the usual pressures and challenges of life.

I've dealt with jealousy and politics in the workplace. Bobby Locke once said, "In all highly competitive sports there is jealousy at the top. Professional golf has its share. Sometimes I think it has more than its share."

Life will hit you harder than a one iron right smack between the eyes.

But here I have learned my lessons, as well. I learned a lot from Lee Trevino, and I have always admired him not only for his excellent golf, but for his character. Lee came from a very poor background, and as a Mexican he also suffered great discrimination. But he never let it get him down. He had an irrepressible nature, and he backed this up with a solid work ethic. He made fortunes with good decisions, lost them with bad decisions, and made them back again. He failed in some areas, as we all have, but I like to think that overall he has succeeded in life. Lee is not a person for regrets. He just gets on with the job of living.

I once asked Lee how he could deal with being so openly discriminated against to the extent of even being told where he could or couldn't sit on a bus. I loved his response, "Gary, a second-class ride is always better than a first-class walk."

When you make your life decisions, try and remember some important golf principles, too. Course management is key, namely, playing what's in front of you, rather than trying to apply your approach to another course.

Celebrate your good decisions and the successes they bring. We don't do this enough. Sometimes I think we go through life making decisions as if our lives literally depend on them. In other words, "If I get this decision right I live. Whew." That's making survival-based decisions.

Or we look at making decisions as a kind of test—get it right, and this door opens to success. Get it wrong, and you're doomed.

I don't have to tell you what putting too much pressure on yourself does to your golf game for you to realize how negatively it will impact your decision-making process, as well.

If you've made a bad decision, accept it as part of the game and something from which you need to learn. It's not the last decision you'll ever make, much like a poor second shot into the rough on a par five is not the last shot you will hit on that hole. You will get another chance to correct that shot. Similarly, you'll get another chance to correct your previous decision.

I also believe in owning your poor decisions.

When I hit a bad shot that puts me in a difficult spot, I accept it as such. I can't go looking for the miracle shot out of the deep rough. Sure, there have been times where I've pulled it off because that shot was on. But if it's not, it would be silly of me to try and force the issue. That's when you just have to take your medicine, and from there your next shot might just be a recovery one to put you back on the fairway, from where you can attack again.

Accept your bad decision as the self-correction that it needs to be. Don't pity yourself. Own it, learn from it, and use it to get better.

Dr. Bob Rotella wrote that great book, *Golf is Not a Game of Perfect*. Similarly, I believe life is not a game of perfect.

Jack Nicklaus and I have often spoken of what you need to do great things in sport, and we always agree—you need to be great yourself. Not great in a boastful sense, but great in self-belief, courage, determination, and all of those good qualities. They are called great things because they require great people.

So what do you need to make the big decisions in your life? You need to be big yourself.

Love the challenges these decisions bring. See them as bringing out the best in you. I did that every time I played Carnoustie in bad weather. Nobody likes that kind of obstacle, but man, I felt like a king every time I knew I'd battled through it and came out on top. Even if coming out on top meant I had to accept shooting a 74 because my nearest competitor shot a 76.

The greatest golfers have always loved the challenge.

Don't make safe decisions. Don't make fearful decisions.

Never be afraid to make a decision. I remember playing golf with Seve Ballesteros and wondering what on earth he was thinking when he hit a certain shot. His decisions seemed to defy logic, and certainly my logic. But he made decisions, and they often worked out to be right for him.

Go ahead and make great decisions.

1. I NEED ADVICE ABOUT SOMETHING, BUT IT FEELS LIKE EVERYBODY I ASK WANTS TO GIVE ME THEIR OPINION RATHER THAN ACTUALLY GIVE ME GOOD ADVICE. WHEN YOU NEED ADVICE, HOW DO YOU HANDLE IT?

Advice is a very tricky thing to give, and to receive.

I once phoned Ben Hogan for advice. He said, "Who do you represent on tour?"

"Dunlop," I said, referring to my sponsor.

"Well, call Mr. Dunlop then" was his curt reply.

Then, as you mentioned, the flip side of the coin is getting advice from everybody when you haven't even asked for it.

There were people very early on in my career, some of them fellow professionals, whose advice to me was to never turn pro because I would starve.

As I've mentioned, even my father was horrified by the prospect of me becoming a golf professional. He also advised me to think twice about my decision.

Or think of all of those times you've maybe hooked your drive and your playing partners are suddenly all experts on the swing, giving you conflicting advice. Most of the time they're no better a golfer than you are. In fact, some of them are sometimes higher handicaps than you.

People love to give advice, but you've got to be careful what advice you accept and what you politely pass over.

I've always felt that if anybody is going to give me advice, they better know more than me regarding the subject on which I'm seeking advice.

For example, if I'm looking for advice on my golf swing, then it's going to be a fellow professional or somebody who plays the game a lot better than I do who I am going to ask.

That's why I don't understand how today's professionals have all these swing coaches who couldn't break 100 on a golf course themselves. Yet the top professionals, Tiger Woods included, place all of their faith in these so-called swing gurus.

I must take a lesson from a guy who can't break 100? Who has never been under pressure to win a Major? Most of whom have never played professional golf?

When I want to invest my money, do you think I take it to my next-door neighbor?

When I was seeking spiritual enlightenment in my life, I spent a lot of time talking to Billy Graham, a great man of his faith.

So make sure you go to the correct source for your advice.

I also believe that there's advice, and then there's everything else, which I like to think of as a tip. Advice is something you take really seriously. A tip is something you can use or discard. When you want advice, don't go to somebody who is just going to give you a tip. As the old joke goes, "I'll give you a tip. Don't run with scissors."

Go out looking for the kind of wisdom you know will add value to your situation. That alone will make you look for the right kind of person qualified to give the right kind of advice.

And don't go to somebody you know is going to tell you what you want to hear. That's not advice. That's looking for a fan. Real advice from a well-intentioned person will challenge you on some level.

It will either challenge you to ignore your doubt about the situation and follow through on what your gut is telling you, or it will challenge you to think more carefully about what you are planning. In the latter case, you probably need to get rid of the emotion you are perhaps feeling at the time and make a decision that is quite possibly not what you had in mind or want to do.

At The Masters a few years ago, Arnold Palmer, Jack Nicklaus, and I were discussing a time in our playing careers when we were considering how best to deal with retirement from the game.

"You didn't call me at all for advice," Jack said to Arnold.

"You called me," said Arnold. "You wanted to go fishing."

"And you haven't taken me up yet."

"I'm going to," replied Arnold.

"OK. Monday?"

"Too soon."

"Jack and I thought we'd retire at 35," I chipped in.

"That's right," said Arnold. "You guys said you were going to quit at 35. I said, 'bullshit.' If I could do it I'd be doing it right now."

I will forever miss Arnold's no-nonsense approach to giving advice.

Advice is like your caddie in life. The caddie who just agrees with you all the time is not worth the golf bag he's carrying.

It's the caddie who sometimes challenges your view, who questions your shot or club choice, whom you value because he's bringing that extra dimension to your thinking.

When I just started playing golf, I'll be the first to tell you that I didn't have a particularly attractive swing. I would hook the ball a lot. The "advice" that people at the time gave me was that I was too small and had a terrible swing to ever consider a serious career in the pro game.

I did my best not to listen to this. But one day I had a particularly bad round. Afterwards I said to my father, "Dad, maybe I'm not good enough to be a champion. Maybe I *am* too small. I can't hit it as far as the other players."

That's when my dad gave me his advice on the matter: "Listen to me. It's about what's inside of you, not what's outside."

Our local golf professional and my future father-in-law, Jock Verwey, also advised me to make a grip change and practice harder.

These were two men I respected and trusted. And most important, they were two men I knew had only my best interests at heart. They had nothing to gain by giving me their advice. But I am so glad I chose to take their advice and ignore the other "advice" of quitting the game altogether.

My father and Jock's advice was designed to help me grow, rather than just make me feel better about myself. It was designed to actually add value to my life and, especially in the case of my father, help me become a better person.

The other "advice" was purely negative. It didn't take into account a person's hard work and determination, or their ability to overcome so much by chasing after their dreams. It was the automatic reaction of people speaking from a position of their own fears and failures instead of speaking to my particular situation.

2. I'M A SUCCESSFUL PROFESSIONAL, BUT I WORRY THAT THROUGH MY SUCCESS I'LL BE SPOILING MY CHILDREN. I GREW UP WITH VERY LITTLE, SO I NATURALLY WANT TO GIVE MY CHILDREN EVERYTHING I COULDN'T HAVE. BUT HOW DO I FIND THE BALANCE BETWEEN HELPING THEM AND SPOILING THEM?

It's a natural thing for us, as parents, to want our children to have better than we had.

One of the reasons why you were successful is because you didn't have much to start with, and that's what you've got to remember.

It would be the wrong attitude to say you want to "give" your children everything, because this would be contrary to the very way you achieved your success.

You've got to have a balance and make sure you don't breed a sense of entitlement in your children. Nobody is entitled to a thing in this world.

There is only the old-fashioned way of earning something.

Given your success, though, your children won't exactly experience all the tribulations and difficulties you encountered because you're living a vastly different lifestyle.

But you've got to learn to say one very important word to them, and that is "No." You can't always be saying "Yes."

When you give them an instruction, they need to learn to adhere to it.

Make sure you teach them about good manners. But most important, make sure they learn gratitude. Make your children realize that they are in the top 1 percent in the world. They cannot grow up believing that what they have is just automatic. You never thought it was automatic. And with all the economic problems facing the world, it's a different time than that during which you grew up, and your responsibility is to make them realize this.

The mistake we often make is that we equate giving our children something to material things.

I grew up poor. I lost my mother to cancer at an early age, so I have always felt a loss in terms of a mother's love. My father had to work long hours to support us, so I was largely left to raise myself. I would wake up early in the morning, with my father already at work in the mines.

We had a wonderful man who worked part-time for us named John Mashaba, and he would make me a bowl of porridge for breakfast. We became good friends. Then I'd walk to the nearest bus stop and catch a bus into town. Once in town, I'd have to transfer to another bus to get to school. After school I'd play my sport, with nobody there to watch me. I often envied the other boys who had their dads on the side of the field or their moms baking cakes for the school. After my school sport I'd catch those two buses home again. And again I'd come home to an empty house. I know my father would dearly have loved to be there, but it just wasn't possible with his work. We needed the money to survive.

But the point is that it made me understand adversity and how this can positively shape a young child's life. It taught me to be independent. It gave me a desire to succeed and an ability to hang tough and overcome challenges.

Naturally, when I had children, I gave them everything I didn't have. Believe me, there are times even now when I tell Vivienne that we have done too much for our kids. I don't mean this in a negative sense. But it's so good for a child to learn a bit of independence. And I've always said that tough times aren't necessarily bad times, and children can learn a lot of lessons from these times.

That being said, you shouldn't feel guilty about your success. What I have tried to do with my own children and grandchildren is to show them the true value of what they have. It's for this reason that we started The Player Foundation. We have managed to raise more than $62 million for underprivileged children worldwide, with the help of generous sponsors and our global Gary Player Invitational tournament series.

Our aim is to reach $100 million in charitable donations, and one of my sons, Marc, is the main driver of this. I'm proud to say that it was he who first had the idea, some 30 years ago, to start a foundation for giving back.

We've built a school on our farm, and our children, as well as our grandchildren, have seen the value of helping the local children to get educated.

When I speak to children who come from well-off families, I always ask them a few questions: "Do you know what a pillow is? Do you know what hot water is? Do you know what a flushing toilet is?" And then I tell them quite clearly, "Consider yourself blessed, because the majority of children worldwide don't have any of these things."

Your children's access to wealth and success is not the evil in this world. It's when it causes them to lose perspective that you need to worry.

I'll never forget speaking to Padraig Harrington at one of our Gary Player Invitationals in South Africa. We had a discussion about exactly this—namely, how do you reconcile the often obscene wealth in professional golf with the challenges and poverty that exist in the real world?

Padraig told me how he'd first experienced this as an amateur. He was staying with the Irish team in a hotel in Calcutta, India. It was a five-star hotel, but he said as soon as they were out the front door they were hit by this incredible poverty.

"It's difficult to play golf in that situation," he said.

Padraig went on to explain how he tried to deal with this.

"You kind of have to compartmentalize it and realize you've got to do your best to help out, even though you can't change the world. But you can help. And then you realize that the best thing I can do is play good golf. If I play good golf then I can afford the time and the money to help others. It's like a lot of things in life. You can't contemplate it too much, for sure. But golf gives us that opportunity. Most professional golfers do something for charity, and what lies behind it is that we're very lucky. We're out there and we're earning large sums of money throughout the year. And to be able to look at yourself in the mirror in the morning you've got to give something back.

"We have to always realize the position we're in and how privileged we are to be doing so well out of it. It would be hard if you just kept taking. It's nice that you can give back. I know from past experience that, at the end of it, we're always the winners. When

I'm on the ground working with people, I'm the one that gets the most out of it. You walk away feeling great."

I couldn't have said it better myself.

I think the difference comes when you realize that what you have is really just on loan to you. The talent and success we have, it's just on loan and it can be taken away tomorrow.

True success is judged by your relationship with your fellow human beings.

With great success comes great responsibility. Show your children how you can be successful and still not forget those around you who are not as fortunate. Give them the gift of counting their blessings every single day. Then give them the vehicle to use success to make a difference in this world.

3. I AM REALLY BAD AT TAKING CRITICISM. WHEN PEOPLE CRITICIZE MY WORK I TAKE IT VERY PERSONALLY. HOW DO YOU HANDLE CRITICISM?

Constructive criticism is one of the finest gifts that you can have bestowed upon you. But it hurts like hell.

Everybody believes that just because I'm such a positive person, I'm somehow immune to criticism.

Well, I'm not. But I have learned over the years to distinguish between good and bad criticism.

Good criticism gets you thinking whether you are right or wrong, and you've got to be humble in your approach and not be militant or rude or arrogant back.

You cannot be emphatic that your opinion is always right.

By working through criticism, we can come to a better conclusion.

Be humble enough to accept criticism and don't take it as you being slighted.

The intention of bad criticism is never to uplift or improve. The person who criticizes you in a negative way has an agenda or an ulterior motive. So it's best to ignore this type of criticism. That doesn't make it any less hurtful though.

I remember when I was playing golf during the apartheid years in South Africa.

Internationally, because I was from South Africa, people branded me a racist. No matter that I did my best to bring about integration in South African golf. I had already started The Player Foundation to help underprivileged children. I had built a school on my farm to help educate the local children, not because I wanted some sort of approval, but because I genuinely believed in trying to help out wherever I could.

But there were those who still wanted to criticize me.

While playing in the United States I lost the PGA Championship one year amidst people shouting during my backswing and throwing ice and telephone books at me.

It didn't matter that I'd personally reached out to the Black Panthers and arranged a meeting just to talk things out so that we could hear each other's side of the story around the race issue in South Africa.

Some people were still determined to criticize me.

Then back home in South Africa, I was walking a similar tightrope. I had a very difficult meeting with the PGA of South Africa regarding its unwillingness to allow black golfers as members. Things became quite heated, and eventually I resigned from the association.

I personally went to see the Prime Minister of South Africa, BJ Vorster, and asked him to allow me to invite the American black professional Lee Elder to come and play in South Africa. This was at a time when Vorster had just banned both black and Asian sportsmen from competing in South Africa. Nevertheless,

Vorster relented to my request. I did my best to support black golfers where I could and helped one of our leading black professionals at the time, Vincent Tshabalala, to travel overseas and play in Europe. I sponsored Papwa Sewgolum for many years, too.

Yet to the liberal left in South Africa I wasn't doing enough to bring down apartheid, while the conservative right criticized me for being a traitor.

I received some tough criticism on the golf course, as well.

As mentioned, I had a pretty rudimentary swing early in my career. On one occasion, I remember playing with Sam Snead in a PGA Tour event. We were tied after regulation play, and then he beat me in a seven-hole playoff. I thought I'd done OK, so afterwards I asked him, "Mr. Snead, is there anything in my swing that you saw which could perhaps help me?" He said, "Son, I ain't seen you swing properly yet."

When I played in my first British Open Championship at St. Andrews in 1955, I hit the worst tee shot of my life on the first, which is known as the widest fairway in golf. It scrambled out of bounds on the right, hit the fence, and fortunately kicked back onto the fairway. As I was walking off the tee, the starter called me over. "Come here, laddie. What's your name?"

"Gary Player, Sir."

"Where you from?"

"South Africa."

"And what's your handicap?"

"I'm a pro."

"You're a pro? You must be a hell of a chipper and putter, because you can't hit the ball worth a damn," he said.

A few years later I became the youngest man at 23 to win The Open. And would you believe it, this same old man was there. He couldn't comprehend it, and I bought him a drink afterwards.

In a strange way though, I consider these examples of positive criticism because there was an element of truth in it. To be honest, I didn't have the best of swings when I started out and I did need to make some changes.

It was the words of men such as these that made me want to work harder, and that inspired me to become better.

You will get criticized throughout your life in whatever you do. And believe me, the more successful you become, the more criticism you will receive. I used to tell my mother-in-law that one day when I'm a world champion everybody will love me. Well, let's just say I'm still learning that this isn't entirely true.

It sounds like such a cliché, but take your criticism whence it comes.

For the rest, treat it as background noise.

I've also found that having the right motives to know that you are only trying to do your best at something is also very helpful in giving you the clarity to spot positive or negative criticism. If the criticism is negative, you will be able to back yourself.

Think of it this way. If you hit a bad shot from a good lie, would you be disappointed with yourself? Of course you would, and you would be right to take this disappointment to heart and use it to improve. And if somebody had to tell you that was a terrible shot, would you be justified in being aggrieved by this assessment? No you wouldn't, because it would be the truth.

But if you hit a bad shot after your opponent purposefully stood on your ball and half buried it, would you still be disappointed with yourself? You might be disappointed with what's happened, but you'd be overly critical if you pointed a finger at yourself for the outcome. Likewise for anybody that unduly criticized you in such a situation. The best thing would be to take it at face value, accept it as something you could do little to change,

and move on. It's not an accurate reflection of your skill, so don't take it to heart.

Often as a young man, when I was criticized, I was inclined to take it too personally.

As you get older you realize, as Shakespeare wrote through the mouth of Polonius in *Hamlet*, "To thine own self be true." I began to sit down and analyze criticism, asking honestly of myself, "Were they right? Was it justified, what they said?"

Criticism gets you thinking, which is good. See it in that light.

And be strong enough to accept it when there is an element of truth in it.

4. I'VE LOST THE PASSION FOR WHAT I DO. HOW DO I GET THAT BACK?

In 1962, I sat on a plane feeling empty.

You know that feeling, the one where your gut feels like it has sunk to the bottom of your shoes, and even breathing feels like an effort.

Everything felt pretty pointless at this stage of my career.

The reason was that I'd suffered golf's version of a sucker punch. And like all sucker punches, I hadn't seen it coming.

When it did, it hit me like a one iron, smack between the eyes at The Open Championship that year. Suddenly, out of nowhere, I felt as if my passion for the game had been snuffed out.

But I need to backtrack a little.

Earlier that year I finished second in The Masters. Now that's hardly a bad result, you might think.

But consider this. I was the defending champion. I'd won the 1961 Masters to become the first international winner of this auspicious tournament. I followed this with a top 10 at the US

Open. But at The Open in 1961, I had to withdraw in the third round because of an upset stomach. It was the first time I'd ever withdrawn from a Major championship, and it would become one of only two occasions in my whole Major career where I had to withdraw from a championship. That was a major mental blow for me because I was only eight strokes off the lead when I had to withdraw. I ended 1961 in a tie for 29th place in the PGA Championship.

So I arrived at The Masters in 1962 keen to get my Major quest back on track.

I led the first round with a 67, and then it was like I just got stuck. Maybe I was stuck mentally, but there were also concerns in terms of my passion.

I couldn't break 71 for the next three rounds. Arnold Palmer shot a 75 in the final round to drop into a playoff with myself and Dow Finsterwald. So in a sense, despite my own frustrations, I was still right in the game.

Then Arnold shot 68 to win the playoff. And you know what I shot in the playoff? 71. For goodness sake, it was like I was golf's version of a hospital flatline that week. I just couldn't get going. I couldn't find that competitive fire.

Then it was off to Oakmont for the US Open. A new week and a new beginning. Guess what. I shot 71 in the first round and another 71 in the second round. I was praying I could just shoot anything besides 71 in a Major championship. Then I did. I shot 72 in the third round and then 74 in the final round, a tale of missed opportunities. Despite my frustrations, I had gone into the final round only two strokes off the lead. But I blew my chances on that final day. So when you read that I finished tied sixth, it doesn't really tell the entire story of where I was mentally at that point in my career.

Then I arrived at the 1962 Open Championship at Royal Troon, and those thoughts of my withdrawal at The Open the previous year were drifting to the surface again.

Troon was running fast and hard, and somehow it all got the better of me.

Continuing with my trend at the US Open, I signed for a first round of 74 and then a second round of 79. I had missed the cut. That was only my second missed cut since I played my first Major at the 1956 Open.

I was devastated. I'd reached the low point of whatever it was that was clouding my mind and robbing me of my passion for the game.

It wasn't just my performances in the Majors that was concerning me. I hadn't won a regular tournament on the PGA Tour either since my 1961 Masters triumph.

I like to say I left Troon with my tail between my legs, because that's how I felt.

I climbed on a plane to America, because in those years the PGA Championship was played only a week after The Open.

I honestly didn't know what I was doing. I felt like a zombie just moving forward but with no idea why or how to get out of the rut I was in.

And the worst part is, I couldn't really say with any certainty what was bothering me.

But the experience at Troon exposed something in me that I didn't like one bit.

At Troon, I reached a point where I just couldn't go on. I was beat, and mentally I was all over the place. The harder I tried, the worse it seemed to get.

I kept playing one particular scene at Troon over and over in my head. It was the par-four 18th. I needed a simple par there to

make the cut. At the back of the 18th green there is out of bounds. A bad bounce, one of so many I'd had that week, saw my ball finish out of bounds, but by only a few inches. It was like the ultimate act of cruelty. I missed the cut by one shot because of that. Man, did I feel cheated by golf and life at that point.

I sat on the plane to America feeling everything from disappointment to anger to resentment. I felt everything, except passion. Around me, my two greatest rivals, Arnold Palmer and Jack Nicklaus, were winning Majors. When you are struggling and around you people are succeeding, it just seems to amplify your own frustration.

I couldn't have won the local club championship thinking the way I was, never mind try and win the PGA Championship.

And that's when I realized I had two choices. I could either carry on down this road of self-pity and intense emotional examination. Or I could change. I could force myself to think more positively about my situation. And that's what I did.

I started telling myself that even though I had never seen Aronimink Golf Club in Pennsylvania, the host of the PGA Championship, I was going to love it. Missing the cut at The Open allowed me to get there earlier than most of the top players. I practiced hard and soaked in everything I could about the course. I phoned the local pro, Joe Capello, and asked if he would play a practice round with me. As one of the local golf writers noted that week, I was going all out to win this one. I played 18 holes a day in practice and worked my tail off on the range until it got dark.

I led with a first round of 72, and then shot 67, 69, and 70 to win by one shot.

My passion was back.

In my life, I've found that the best way of rekindling my passion for my game or career is to stay with the process, but not to

fight it. Some people might step away from things to try and gain perspective, and this can also work. But I'm a worker by nature, so I've always felt that by staying with the process and working through it, or more to the point letting it work through you, I've always managed to get back on track.

If I'd walked away after The Open at Troon, there would've been nothing forcing me to make that change in my head. I would've gone home and stewed with those same negative emotions.

Sometimes a little bit of pressure to change helps kick-start the passion again.

So my advice would be to stick with the process and almost befriend it to the extent of, as I mentioned earlier, letting it work through you. Don't try and understand it. Don't try and figure it out or have all the answers. And please don't get stuck with those negative emotions. Often you won't know why you feel the way you do, or what the solution is. You may, just like me, need to stay in that moment and put one foot in front of the other until that spark comes along that reignites your passion for what you do.

5. DO YOU HAVE A PROCESS FOR MAKING DECISIONS?

Not really.

As mentioned earlier, though, I do have a lot of factors I like to consider as part of my decision-making process.

When it comes to making big decisions, I never want to be in a hurry.

Now I admit this is not always possible. Sometimes we are under pressure to make a decision, and then you need to go with what you feel and accept that your life and experience has prepared you for this.

In 1964, my late brother Ian and I went on a fishing trip in the Zululand region of South Africa. It was one of the most spectacular and memorable trips we ever took together.

When it was over, on the day we left we had to drive for miles along the beach. At one point we got stuck and Ian's Land Rover began to get pounded by the waves. We quickly jumped out and had to start digging for all we were worth to free the tires. Ian said he was amazed by how calm I was throughout it all. He said later that he could see how years of being in tense situations on the golf course had taught me to move quickly and make snap decisions calmly. But if you can, give yourself a little time to think, because what you think today is very different from what you think tomorrow.

So have patience.

Then, whenever I have a big decision to make, I always ask the opinions of my wife, Vivienne, and my son, Marc.

I may also consult some of my close friends who have been very successful in life in order to come up with an overall opinion.

I also prioritize my decisions.

I really don't want to be stuck obsessing about what I'm going to have for breakfast, so that's why I keep it simple and healthy and I stick to that.

If I'm going to be making decisions, then I want to save my mental energy for the decisions that really matter.

This world is full of distractions. There are so many things that can pull your thoughts away from the important decisions you need to make.

Distraction is a killer when it comes to making decisions. The world will tell you everything demands your attention and everything is important. But deciding whether or not to respond to a Facebook friend request is really not as important as you are being led to believe. It's certainly not as important as deciding to which school to send your kids.

I also try to never make a decision based on fear. I accept that I may be emotionally invested in a decision, and I know it sounds like a cliché, but I never want to make a decision when I'm emotional.

And I never want to approach a decision with the belief that I am faced with either a right or a wrong choice. Sure, jumping into a fire involves a very clear right and wrong choice. But the decisions of life are usually a lot more subtle than this.

I have found, in many of my decisions, that I could have gone either way and still had a satisfactory result. In making my decision I was looking for the best result of two good ones.

My advice would be to develop your decision-making process like you would put together a set of golf clubs for yourself.

You'll find clubs you hit really well compared to others. Your driver may differ vastly from your irons. Your putter may not be the latest technology, but it gets the job done for you like nothing else. And that's how you build up your golf bag for the challenges you will face on the course. I think you can do the same with your decision-making process in pooling all of your resources and using everything that is available to make your decision.

6. I'VE HAD SEVERAL SETBACKS IN MY LIFE. HOW DO YOU KEEP PICKING YOURSELF UP WHEN THINGS GO WRONG?

Perspective, attitude, and faith.

Perspective to realize that you're not the only one who's had setbacks in life. Everybody who has put their feet on this earth has setbacks.

When you have setbacks and you handle them in a positive way, you improve on things and you become better.

Look at the setbacks some of the greatest people in history have had. Look at Winston Churchill, one of my all-time heroes. In the 1930s he was languishing in the political wilderness because of his outspoken views on certain manners. Yet just a few years later he would lead the free world in the most important battle of the age as they sought to withstand the might of Nazi Germany. Thousands of lives were being lost all around him. Cities and countries risked being destroyed by one wrong decision. Those are unimaginable consequences to have to consider.

And then, having showed tremendous leadership and courage and having helped the Allies to win the war, he was tossed onto the political scrapheap shortly after again. Yet he remains one of the greatest figures in history.

So when it has come to the biggest disappointments or saddest moments in my life—of which there have been many—I have always tried to maintain perspective.

Yes, I am an optimist. But optimism alone does not pick you up off the floor. It's a bit like telling somebody who suffers from chronic depression that they simply need to shake themselves right and think positively.

No, when somebody sinks as low as that really dark mental place, a few clichéd sayings just won't cut it.

I've always found that perspective is a lens through which I'm able to better view and as such deal with my disappointment or suffering.

For starters, I accept that it's okay to feel disappointed, defeated, or just plain sad. We are human beings, not machines. We feel, as much for others as for ourselves.

Ignoring your feelings would be to ignore the very thing that makes us human and distinguishes us from every other living creature.

But giving in to our feelings or being ruled by them is where we get it wrong.

Accept how you feel about a situation, but as part of a process that gets you back to where you feel positive and confident again.

Never get stuck in that moment.

Self-pity is one of the most devastating emotions from which a human being can suffer. It's utterly debilitating and destructive.

My advice would be to take your feelings for what they are and then use them to move forward.

The human experience of physical pain is designed exactly for this purpose. We cannot ignore pain because it plays a very important role in keeping us alive.

When we hurt ourselves physically, our brain responds by creating the feeling of pain as a means of alerting us to the danger. If it did not, we'd all wipe ourselves out without ever knowing it.

So pain is good because we learn from it. Even as children we learn that if we touch a hot stove it will hurt. But to just sit there, lament the pain, and vow never to go near a stove again or ever cook a meal would be silly.

I've seen some very real hurt and pain in people over the years, and I've lived through it myself.

This includes people who suffer with terrible disease or circumstances beyond their control, and people who just get knocked down by a myriad of unfortunate events that have left me wondering when that poor soul is going to get a good break in life.

I recently visited Japan and I spoke with a girl who lost everything in the 2011 earthquake and tsunami. By everything, I mean her parents, her grandparents, her sibling, and even her beloved dog. She was quite literally alone in the world. What unbelievable sadness to have to deal with as a child. But she had the most positive attitude.

I spend a lot of time visiting townships in South Africa and speaking to the children there. A lot of them are neglected. Many of them have been physically and emotionally abused. Then I look back on my own childhood. I grew up without a mother and was largely left on my own. Was it hard? Of course it was. Was it as hard as some other children have it? No, it was not. I'm not suggesting that you take some sort of perverse satisfaction in the fact that somebody else is suffering more than you. But perspective allows you to understand that what you may think is a terrible situation is perhaps not as bad in the bigger scheme of things.

And then we come to faith. My faith is strong and I believe is in control of all things, including my life. It's why I have always stated that my talent for golf is on loan to me. It's not something for which I can ever take credit. It was a gift given to me that I had to work hard to take advantage of.

Similarly, I believe that through all the good and the bad, the success and the suffering, a strong faith will allow you to work through it all with courage, dignity, and conviction.

So how do I pick myself up when I've had the emotional stuffing knocked out of me?

Well, I take one step. It may be a physical or an emotional one. But I take that first step forward. And then I take another. And another. And I keep moving. I may not see or understand where I'm moving to. But I keep moving forward, because to stand still and remain in that place of disappointment or hurt will break you.

Sometimes on my farm in the Karoo of South Africa we have to clear great areas of veld to plant something. I enjoy physical labor, so I often help out. At first you just see this mess of bushes and weeds and rocks and you're left a little intimidated at the sheer scale of the job at hand. And even when you start clearing it feels like you're making very little progress. You can't imagine what the end result will look like because you're just focused on the next tough little thorn bush in front of you. Your hands and back hurt, the sun beats down on you, and the sweat gets in your eyes, but you just keep hacking away. Then you look up and see what you have cleared, and suddenly you can start to see a small piece of field where you are going to plant some vegetables. What you couldn't see before is now a very real prospect right in front of you.

I don't know what your setbacks are. They could be physical, financial, or emotional.

But my advice is to have faith in the goodness of life. Don't ignore your emotions. Use them to help you understand your situation and to guide you through it. Believe that you will get through this, and the next challenge, and the next one after that.

An optimist is not somebody who simply wills himself to see life as a bed of roses and then believes it is so. That's a head-in-the-sand approach to life.

An optimist is somebody who understands the challenge and knows there will be heartache, but who has an unshakeable belief in his or her ability to handle it with dignity and overcome it.

Believe not in your ability to avoid trouble and strife.

Believe in your ability to get through it.

7. HOW DO YOU FIND THAT BALANCE BETWEEN DOING WHAT YOU LOVE AND PURSUING YOUR DREAMS, BUT ALSO BEING REALISTIC AND NOT CHASING A FAIRY TALE?

When I said I was going to become a world champion, I was determined to let nothing stand in my way.

I don't think that I had any more natural talent than the next person. But I did know that I was prepared to work harder than anybody else to achieve my dream of playing professional golf, winning the biggest tournaments, and becoming the best in the world.

So much of the great achievements throughout history have started out as people chasing what many believed were unrealistic dreams.

I think what it boils down to is how badly do you want it.

But when does a dream or goal become, as you put it, simply chasing an unrealistic fairy tale?

In professional sports, this line becomes a lot clearer by the very nature of being a professional.

It begins with your love for the sport and then a dream to make this your career. When you turn professional, you still have dreams, but you have to balance these with the very real need to earn a living.

For example, by 1956, I had made quite a good start to my professional career with a number of wins. It was now my dream to play in a Major championship, in particular The Masters at Augusta National. But I needed two things—first an invitation, and second the money to get there.

Unbeknownst to me, my father wrote a letter to the then-chairman of Augusta National Golf Club, Clifford Roberts, in which he said, "If you could extend my son an invitation to The Masters, I will pass the hat here in Johannesburg and obtain the necessary funds."

The response from Roberts was, "Pass the hat."

In 1957, I made my Masters debut and finished tied 24th. To this day, I am very proud to have won the event three times and played it on a record 52 occasions.

But you see a lot of cases in professional golf where players reach a point in their careers where it hasn't yet happened for them, and they need to make a decision.

That's when a professional might start thinking of the song by Kenny Rogers where he sings about knowing when to hold onto a good hand or to walk away from a bad one.

But when you've been chasing a dream for so long, it becomes very difficult to let it go.

And there is also an argument to be made as to whether you should let it go. I've also seen many professional golfers grind it out for years with very little reward and then *bang!*—their week comes and they win a Major.

But of course there are countless other tales of players who just never get that one magical week. They might also have to start thinking about other ways to earn a living, especially if they have a family to support.

And then there's the other scenario where you wonder how many great talents have been lost by people quitting too soon and not seeing that balance between getting through a hard patch, and realizing that this is more than just a stumbling block and they may have to think of another career.

So where is the secret?

I think you need to be very honest with yourself.

You need to know if your dream is achievable. You can dream about flying like Superman, but unless the law of gravity suddenly changes, you're never going to achieve it. You can also dream of playing the piano like a concert pianist. Even if you've never played piano before, with enough hard work and practice you might be able to achieve that dream. But you will have to make massive sacrifices that you need to be comfortable making.

You also need to be honest enough to accept that your dream might require some modification along the way.

As a professional golfer, it may be that you need to shift your focus from playing the Tour to working in golf as a club professional or coach. You're still involved in what is your passion, just in a different area that may be more suited to you and your talents.

If your dream depends on your ability to eventually earn a living from it, then you have to be honest about this, as well.

You've quantified your dream as a means of providing money for you. It's now no longer just a passion you have. It has gone beyond being something you do in your spare time, and which you may do very well. You have now labeled your dream as being required to earn you a living. If it doesn't, then there is a problem with your dream.

It doesn't mean that you have to stop dreaming about becoming a world champion surfer. But you need to find a way to fund it if you're going to keep at it.

I think that's a very important thing for parents to remember in this age where becoming a professional sportsman or sportswoman is so desirable.

As a parent, it doesn't help that you instantly kill a child's dream in this area if you believe they won't be able to earn a living from it.

The better way is to be honest with your child and say, "Right, you want to be a professional sportsman. Well, let's work out how you're going to earn a living so you can chase that dream."

A dream is something you can keep chasing if you've identified concrete steps on your journey and thought it through beyond just the very easy part of saying, "I want to do this . . ."

A dream is not just some flight of fancy or a spark in your imagination. It may begin there, but a real dream is something you think very hard about and make plans to achieve. To keep making plans (very real plans in a very real world) and keep finding a way is what keeps a dream alive, and at the same time achievable.

A fairy tale needs the presence of a fairy to make it real. Apart from my lovely wife Vivienne, I haven't seen too many fairies in this world.

Once you are on the path to achieving that dream, it is important to keep focused.

I've seen a few golfers in my time who were brilliant. They were achieving. They were successful. They were highly talented and they were on a path to being great. But then they started tinkering with their swings in the belief that they could be better. And suddenly they dropped out of the game and were never heard from again.

The mistake they made was chasing a fairy tale and not staying with their dream. They went beyond what they were capable of. They failed to realize that perhaps where they were was as good as they could be, and that they should enjoy that success. They thought they could be better and then realized that they couldn't. They chased the fairy tale, and that's when the dream became a nightmare.

I suppose if you look at my own career, the pursuit of my dream involved doing the best with what I had to become a golf professional. My version of chasing a fairy tale would have involved trying to hit the ball farther than that of bigger and stronger players such as Jack Nicklaus and Arnold Palmer, and to stop focusing on my strengths of being a hard worker in all areas of my own game.

That would have been a mistake, though. Everybody needs to realize their capabilities and live accordingly.

You've got to be realistic about things. You've got to know your talents. Confide in your family or your friends who know you well and can tell you if you're being realistic or not.

8. THERE IS SO MUCH CONFLICTING ADVICE AROUND NUTRITION. WHAT'S YOUR TAKE ON IT, AND WHAT DIET WOULD YOU ADVISE?

Years ago I played a series of challenge matches in New Zealand with David Thomas, Harold Henning, and Peter Thomson. We played 26 matches in 30 days.

At the end of it I wanted to unwind in a big way. I asked David to start mixing the strongest drinks he could and to keep them coming. The next day I felt like death and resolved never to do that again. I haven't.

I also tried smoking once. It was a pipe. But afterwards my mouth felt like the bottom of a birdcage, so that was the end of that.

My point is that I've learned what is good for my body and what isn't.

There are so many fads when it comes to diets, a lot of it designed to make money out of nutrition.

Thus, it's hard to know what to eat and what to avoid.

Right now we're being told to avoid carbohydrates and eat meat. Well, while I agree on not eating too many carbohydrates, I'm not so sure about too much meat, either.

I try and stay away from too much of anything.

Red meat could well have steroids in it. Chicken could have antibiotics in it. And when you consider that five billion people's waste goes into the ocean every day, every bit of fish you eat has a little of that in it, too.

So I stick to eating as much organic food as I can with a good balance between protein, vegetables, and fruit.

I also have a few of my own golf rules of nutrition. The one is to eat less sugar. Everybody seems to be in agreement that sugar is a great killer and a cause of multiple issues in the body.

I also try and avoid cold meats, or processed meats. The World Health Organization (WHO) recently came out saying it is one of the biggest causes of cancer. Much information is conflicting, confusing, and biased.

I've experimented with diet and nutrition all my life because I believe that one of the secrets to being a great athlete is to find ways to eat better.

The worst thing you can do, which is very prevalent in our society, is to overeat. Everybody eats way too much, in my opinion. The less you eat, the longer you live. Why do we have to be slaves to this three-square-meals-a-day type of thinking? Some days you need only one meal, and some days you may need three.

My best advice would be to have a good breakfast, a nice lunch, and a small dinner. You don't have to put gasoline in your car when you park it in the garage at night. And when you're sleeping at night, you don't need food. You're lying on your bed and it's hard to digest that food because you're not exercising or moving.

I'd also strongly recommend you start your day eating greens. We don't eat enough greens. There are many children in the world who don't even know what greens are. When I was a young boy I used to eat marog, which is a South African version of spinach. Most days my choice is a mixed greens smoothie from our garden.

I've been a meat eater and a vegetarian in my life, and I can honestly say that every year of my life I have learned to eat better.

I can also say without a doubt that the traditional Western diet is criminal. It should be outlawed, for goodness sake.

I know there is a big move now toward the low carbohydrate, high fat (LCHF) diet, but frankly most people have no idea what the difference is between good fat and bad. I have always tried to limit the animal fat intake in my body. I love avocados though, which is a source of the kind of good fats and oils you should be eating.

Going back to sugar, I think if you are looking to make one big and immediate change to your health and nutrition, then start here.

It will instantly make a world of difference to your quality of life. I'm not just talking about being able to avoid such dreaded diseases as diabetes, but rather your general state of health. By eliminating sugar you'll find your body has a much more natural rhythm to it, and you won't experience those sudden highs and lows throughout the day.

When I say eliminate sugar, I know we are all going to pop a sweet into our mouths at some point. I even have a secret little stash of chocolate that my staff refers to as my medicine pack. Or you'll be at a party where you're offered a slice of cake. The aim is not to turn you into some Spartan individual with no sense of humor sitting in a corner snacking on a broccoli stick.

Rather, it's to make sure you eliminate the sustained sugar in your diet.

I generally try and eat as close to a vegetarian as possible. I'm trying to eat more like a vegan actually, but I haven't reached that point yet. I do love a great steak, grilled salmon, or piece of chicken occasionally.

Generally I stick to a plant-based diet, which I supplement with nuts and fruit.

This is purely because I know it makes me feel good.

For breakfast I might have some fruit or even some oatmeal. And I always start the day with my famous green juice. The recipe for it is as follows:

2 spinach leaves
1 kale leaf
Juice of a half lemon
Small piece of ginger
1 apple
½ a cucumber
1 piece of celery

Stick that all into a blender and drink it first thing in the morning. You'll feel incredible.

Whatever I eat, I try and eat as close to organic as possible. I try and follow the rule to eat as close to the earth as possible, or as close to the source. Get rid of the junk food and takeaways. It's all processed poison.

I'm not saying my diet will necessarily work for you. But I would advise that you think more carefully about what you eat. Balance and moderation have worked best for me.

For generations we've just eaten according to tradition. We wouldn't dream of putting substandard petrol into our cars that could harm the engine, yet we're quite happy to stuff any old thing into our bodies. And then we wonder why we get sick or can't perform at our best.

Now more than ever we have access to quality food and the information to help us make better eating choices. All it takes is the will and some planning.

If you are looking to switch to a more vegetarian diet, I'd suggest you first do your research.

Changing the way you eat and being able to sustain this will only work if you believe in what you are doing. You need to buy into it to be able to keep at it.

Then I'd suggest you start with small changes. Making a whole-sale change overnight is just going to frustrate you because you will have cravings for your old diet. Ease yourself into this new way of eating.

Your diet will not be perfect all of the time, just like every day of work is not a perfect one. You will have moments when you eat that chocolate cake or grab a fizzy cold drink. But the point is to make these the exception. I once read a nutrition article by the big wave surfer Laird Hamilton in which he said he likes to think of his body as a diesel truck. Sometimes a bit of substandard diesel will get in there, but while the truck might splutter a bit it will still keep on going. I think that's a very nice analogy for the balance that is required.

You know, sometimes I think we eat so badly purely because we've given ourselves so many food choices. Most middle-class families throw away more food than they can eat. I think it's time to get back to the basics of what works well in your body.

Though I acknowledge this move to a high-fat diet and how some are promoting it as the cure for all sorts of bodily ailments, I'm not fully convinced after doing a bit more research on the subject. I still prefer to lean more heavily toward a plant-based diet. On my farm in the Karoo I have the most incredible vegetable garden, from which we all eat.

Plus, I abide by my belief that we often eat from a base of tradition rather than a real need to satisfy hunger. Thus, I try to eat less rather than more, and I'm not rigid about meal times.

Do your research. Know where your food comes from. Figure out what foods make you feel good. Drink enough high-quality water (there is a difference) and keep flushing out your system as much as possible.

If some of it sounds simple, that's because it is. Get rid of the sugar, be militant regarding carbohydrates and not eating too much of them, and drink water daily. These three things alone will add immeasurably to your overall well-being and nutritional health.

Remember, eat healthy to make it a lifestyle. Don't just get on some diet to lose a few pounds. It won't last.

Your body is the greatest gift you have been given. If you want to be productive in this world you've got to have a good body. You've got to have energy, and you build energy by exercising, resting well, being happy and laughing, and eating correctly.

I don't expect the average person to exercise like I do as a professional sportsman. But just at least go for a daily walk. Buy yourself a treadmill if you must. Just start walking for a mere 15 minutes a day.

Use your body well, treat it well, and like me it will reward you well into your old age. Rest is rust. Keep moving.

9. HOW DO YOU HANDLE CONFLICT WITH YOUR PEERS?

I have always taken great pride in being honest and truthful, but I have been called a cheat in my career. That's what a leading golf professional called me. Not once. Twice.

After the 1974 Open Championship at Royal Lytham, a player dropped a bombshell when he accused me of cheating. I was blown away by the accusation that I had played another ball on the 17th.

I had been six strokes ahead at the time and had hit my ball over the back of the green into the thick rough. I never thought we'd find the ball. I immediately asked a rules official to put me on the clock so I could observe the five-minute rule when looking for a lost ball. My caddie found the ball, I made a bogey five, and I went on to win. Only after the championship, when I had left the golf course, did the player make the accusation that I had played another ball that was not my original ball. Then came the accusations that my caddie, Alfred "Rabbit" Dyer, had dropped another ball.

The fact that there were TV cameras on us the whole time, and the fact that we had rules officials and members of the gallery helping us search for the ball, seemed lost on those who thought the player had a case. How would it have been possible with all those eyes on us for Rabbit to suddenly drop another ball for me to play? Rabbit himself denied this in many interviews, saying exactly the same thing. He agreed that it just wasn't possible to do with all the attention on us at the time. But Rabbit did perhaps explain where the rumors came from. He said that earlier in the week, when he was walking the golf course for yardages, a couple of the English caddies cornered him and started calling him "Nigger" and telling him to leave and go home back to the USA. One of them grabbed him and Rabbit punched him, knocking him down. One of the papers got wind of the story and ran it under the headline, "Sugar Ray Rabbit knocks caddie out."

This player also accused me of going seven seconds over the five minutes given to search for the ball. And he did all of this after the fact. The correct procedure is to report an incident immediately after play. There's even a theory that my original ball was later found and is sitting in a safe somewhere. In a safe? Where? Whose safe? How has it been identified as mine?

Then in a Skins game in Arizona in 1983, a player accused me of cheating. He said that I had flattened out a rooted leaf behind my ball on the 16th hole before playing a chip shot. It became a very public issue that was reported in the newspapers.

We had a meeting with rules officials about it, and upon further review of the video, it was agreed that I had done nothing wrong. The player thought he saw me flatten the rooted leaf to improve my lie. The reality is that I bent down, looked at it, and gently moved it to see if it was attached. It was, and therefore I left it. Again, the TV cameras were on me at the time.

But when I went to discuss the matter with the player and Joe Dey, the player also suddenly brought up an incident during a Canadian tournament we played in where he allegedly refused to sign my scorecard because he claimed I had tapped down a spike mark on the green. The allegation was that PGA Tour officials had to sign my card because this player refused to. I remembered the incident because when I first heard the rumor, I immediately phoned Clyde Mangum, the PGA official who was in charge of that event. He was just as astonished as I was. "I have no knowledge of this, Gary," he said. "You signed your card. So did the other player." I later challenged this player on it, and he denied that any such incident had occurred. So when we met with Joe Dey over the Skins game incident, I went so far as to ask that the TV broadcasters replay the film to prove I had done nothing wrong. I was particularly hurt that in these accusations the correct procedures were not followed.

For me, the resolution of sometimes inevitable conflict with peers boils down to communication.

We need to be more humble, be more receptive, and communicate better. It takes a real person to admit they are wrong. Be courageous and admit when you make a mistake.

When you look at the great figures in history, such as a man like Nelson Mandela, you realize that these people could admit when they were wrong, even though they weren't wrong very often.

Nobody likes conflict, but it's unavoidable in this life. It's human nature that you're not going to get along with everybody all of the time.

Disagreements in life are one thing and will obviously happen. Arguments are also commonplace. But what I have never appreciated is a lack of honesty when it comes to such disagreements. If I have made a mistake, call me on it right there and then, and let's deal with it properly.

When this doesn't happen is when the issue becomes personal.

If you have created the conflict with your peers—either willingly or unwittingly—then set it straight in an open and honest way.

If they are creating the conflict, take it up with them directly.

When you're honest, then you're not embarrassed to face your peers in a conflict situation. It's when you've got something to hide or have an ulterior motive that you will find it difficult to deal with.

And if their conflict with you stems from their jealousy of you, then respond to them in love.

In later years I tried my best to respond to conflict situations with love.

I also find that when it comes to conflict, and this may sound clichéd, take the high road, my friend. I'm not saying avoid conflict or try and run away from it. What I'm saying is keep the moral high ground. No matter how ugly it becomes or how personal the other individual gets, stay away from that and stick to the facts of the situation.

The reason I say this is that you will be better for it.

When people allow themselves to sink to the level of the attack they're facing, that's when things get messy for all concerned.

Next minute you're both throwing so much mud at each other that you're both dirty.

And what people often find so difficult about conflict, in the workplace especially, is that they have to face that person every day. It becomes uncomfortable, doesn't it?

But if you have kept the moral high ground, you have nothing to be embarrassed about. You can respond to that person with respect and love, and with your own head held high.

You are in control of that situation. You may not always win the argument, but you have won the emotions surrounding it all.

You will be in control of yourself. When I look in the mirror, I know the truth.

10. I'M TERRIFIED OF SPEAKING IN FRONT OF PEOPLE. HOW DO YOU DO IT?

I'm ashamed to say that I wasn't a very good student. I just never studied hard enough.

I've since come to realize how important academics are in life.

I was very much an average student. I think I could've been a better student, but I just didn't work hard at my academics.

Of all my school subjects, I loved Geography the most. I didn't like History, although today I am very fond of it. I enjoyed English, but for an entirely different reason than you would think.

My dad used to say to me, "Gary, if you're going to be a world champion, then you'd better learn how to speak well." So I embraced English and worked hard at it.

I was fascinated by the great orators of the world, such as Winston Churchill, Mohatma Gandhi, John F. Kennedy, Abraham Lincoln, and later Nelson Mandela.

I would study their speeches and how they spoke.

When I started winning tournaments, I realized very quickly how important it was to be able to speak well in public.

To this day I am very proud of the fact that whenever I was interviewed by journalists I always gave them more than what they asked for.

In short, I knew how important it was for me to communicate well in front of people, so I made work of it. I practiced. And just like my golf, the harder I practiced, the luckier I became.

You could argue that I was already a public figure by virtue of playing golf in front of an audience, so maybe I was more used to being in front of people, which made speaking in front of them easier.

But I know of many golfers who are quite comfortable playing in front of a crowd but are less so speaking in front of one.

It always astounds me how today's young professionals have everything from sports psychologists to fitness and nutrition experts at their disposal, but not one of them has anybody teaching them effective communication.

It's a vital part of their jobs that they are able to speak well and convey important messages through the media. Yet so many professional athletes are poor speakers. They don't make an effort to improve their word power, or listen to great speakers and try to learn from them.

However, if I can give you one piece of advice, for heaven's sake don't follow the old adage of imagining all the people in the room naked to put you at ease. I don't know about you, but speaking to a room full of naked people would make me even more anxious.

I think what also helps me is that when I stand up in front of people, I don't try and manufacture speeches. I just speak from my heart, like I'm talking to my friends.

I have a love for people. I love meeting people and interacting with people. I love to hear their stories. And I love and appreciate the opportunity I have of perhaps influencing or inspiring people.

So I think this has also helped me with my public speaking.

I've also found that it's vital to be yourself. As much as I admired the oratory skills of the gentlemen I have mentioned, I also realized that I was not them. I had to speak like myself. I had to stay true to my beliefs and not try and be Winston Churchill when I spoke.

Be yourself and see your opportunity to speak as a genuine chance to share with the people in front of you. Don't see them as there to judge what you are going to say. See them as your fellow human beings with whom you badly want to share information.

And then tell them your story.

Don't try and use words you wouldn't normally use. Don't try and throw in all sorts of facts and figures you know nothing about. Just keep it real.

The best public speaking is speaking that comes from the heart.

That's the kind of speaking that touches people.

And don't misinterpret a few nerves as being a fear of public speaking.

Everybody has nerves. I had nerves every time I played in a Major. Nerves are good. They keep you sharp.

So just be yourself.

We have nothing more to give this world than who we are. So give the best of yourself, and I guarantee you that will be better than any fabricated version of yourself you think people want to hear when you address them.

11. I FEEL LIKE I'M NOT DOING WHAT I WAS MADE FOR. HOW DID YOU FIND YOUR PURPOSE IN LIFE?

From a very early age I knew I wanted to be a world champion, but I couldn't tell you that I knew right from the start that it would be in golf.

My father played a bit of golf, and I always looked at it as most young people do—as a game for older men.

I was naturally drawn to the outdoors and sports. My brother Ian helped fuel this passion in me. So I suppose you could say I was always destined to do something involving the outdoors and physical activity.

I was a good sportsman at school and played most sports, including rugby and cricket, where I also excelled. I was also a keen swimmer and track athlete.

Through sports, I found a means to prove a point.

I was small and short, and for a time I believed all the naysayers and bullies who told me I was too short for certain sports.

Then my brother started to influence my thinking and challenged me to prove them wrong.

So I would train for the 100 meters, determined to beat those boys who called me a shorty. And I did.

Sport was a way for me to prove a point, perhaps more to myself than anybody else, that I did indeed have a purpose in life.

It was only later that I discovered golf and found a passion for it after my first round at Virginia Park Golf Club in Johannesburg.

Then, all of those same qualities of wanting to prove how good I could be and the determination to work hard to show the world I could be a world champion naturally came through, as well.

Was I destined to become a world-class golfer?

I don't know.

I like to think that I had all the attributes—including a willingness to work hard and suffer if need be—that would've made me successful at whichever sport I chose.

Except high diving.

It was an attempt at high diving into a pile of leaves at my high school that saw me almost break my neck and very nearly ended my sports career for good. It was meant to be a prank and I can laugh about it now. High diving definitely works better into a pool than a pile of leaves.

The point I'm making is that finding your purpose is a journey.

Sometimes it can be as clear as day, and you may wake up with a vision of exactly who you are and what you are meant to do in this life.

But my experience with myself and others is that it's more a journey of self-discovery.

Think about the many people who get on trains early in the morning when it's still pitch-dark and cold, to go and sew buttons on shirts in a factory.

How about people like my father who worked miles underground in a gold mine? How many people enjoy their work in the world? Very few. But unfortunately we don't all have a choice to enjoy our work. Some of us are just lucky enough to have a job, and hundreds of millions of people just want the same.

So you can adjust your mind to make yourself realize how fortunate you are to have a job. Work hard at it, and if you find something along the way that you feel you can do better at, then devote your time to it. But don't let things get out of context in your own mind.

As was the case with me, you may have a general aptitude for something, and within that could be a myriad of paths you choose to take.

I would say start with trying to identify that general passion you have, that thing within you that you know makes you different from the person next to you. From there you can begin looking at what options the world offers in these areas, and slowly working your way toward something where you know you can make a difference.

Don't try and start with the end in mind, namely, trying to pinpoint the exact job or career you think is your calling in life.

It's a bit like playing a golf hole.

You stand on the tee knowing that you can hit a golf ball and you can hit it well, but the fairway before you presents you with a number of places where you can hit that golf ball. It's up to you to then choose where you want to hit it.

Trying to decide where you are gong to hit the ball before you've even seen the hole is futile. In golf we talk about playing what's in front of you.

Always remember that finding your purpose in life should be a wonderful journey.

As human beings we are so results-oriented. There is a place for this in the world because that's what moves humanity forward as a whole.

But when it comes to the individual, don't be so focused on finding your purpose that it defines your entire existence to the point that you lose your pleasure for everything else in life.

If you feel like you are not doing what you were made for, well, that's a good thing because it's the first step on your journey toward understanding your purpose. But it's a journey, not a lucky dip packet you simply stick your hand into one day and then pull out a purpose.

Understand it for what it is and embrace this, while never losing sight of the day-to-day wonder of life in all of its glorious creativity.

12. HOW DID YOU DEAL WITH MAJOR CRISIS POINTS IN YOUR LIFE?

When I was 8 years old, I saw my mother for the last time. It was on Christmas Day.

My father had taken my sister, Wilma, and me to visit my mom in the hospital where she was fighting cancer. She was in so much pain.

She had been diagnosed with cancer about 18 months before. She'd had a mastectomy, but the cancer kept spreading. Eventually it ended up in her spine.

I saw her that Christmas Day, and she died two days later.

Eight years old, and suddenly the world you know is ripped from under you.

It was a time of immense turmoil for our family.

To this day my sister sobs her heart out at Christmas.

Even for me, Christmas is a time filled with so many memories that I've spent a lifetime trying to control and deal with.

You see, something also broke in me that day my mom died. Something that I have spent the rest of my life trying to fix, and even trying to replace with my achievements on the golf course.

Whenever I won tournaments I would feel it was my way of proving to my mom that I'd done good and she could be proud of me, even though she wasn't there to see it.

I would wake up crying in the middle of the night just thinking of her. To this day if I see a photograph of my mom, the tears start to flow.

It was particularly bad during the 1965 US Open. I'd won my fourth Major. Here I was, 29 years old and only the third person in history to win the career Grand Slam—all four Majors— and the first foreigner to do so after the American greats Gene Sarazen and Ben Hogan. It should have been the greatest time of my life.

But I woke up in the middle of almost every night of that tournament crying like a baby because I missed her so much.

There is not a day that goes by that I don't think about her. And it's always the same dream. I see my mom. I call out to her. But she can't hear me. I try to tell her what I've achieved, how successful I've become, how proud she can be of me. But she never hears me.

That crisis point in my life, of losing my mother so early on, had a profound impact on my identity at the time.

At school the other kids used to call me shorty, which you wouldn't think is such a bad thing. After all, kids call one another names on the playground all day long. But it used to hurt me deeply because I already felt like an outsider as a result of not having a mom there supporting me like the other boys did, or baking cakes for them.

I've had other crisis points in my life. I've lost my brother, the renowned conservationist Dr. Ian Player, and had to deal with that late in my life. He was such a big influence on me and shaped the competitive spirit I have.

I was also not there the day he died. I did see him one last time before he passed away, though, much like my mom.

I sat by his bedside. His eyes were closed, and I wasn't even sure he could hear me. I held his hand. "Brother, if you can hear me, just squeeze my hand," I whispered to him.

I thought about my big brother. The one I always looked up to. The one who used to beat me in races and would then literally kick my butt for not trying hard enough. He squeezed my hand one last time.

I've had severe injuries that have threatened my career. In 1972 I had to undergo surgery for some major kidney problems. I've struggled with neck trouble during my career as well from an old school injury.

I've had business challenges. Family challenges. I've had the major crises you would expect from life, and which millions of people suffer on a daily basis.

How do I deal with it?

There is no plan for those moments that quite literally shake our worlds.

I've been to countries where people have been ravaged by war and disease. I've sat in shacks in townships where people have nothing of value but the smiles on their faces.

But you will get through it, and it's important to remember this.

It doesn't make the experience any less hurtful or tough to deal with. But you will get through it. It will leave its mark on you for sure, as does everything in this world. But you will get through it.

Remember this.

13. I'M A "YES" MAN, AND IT OFTEN PUTS IMMENSE PRESSURE ON ME. HOW CAN I LEARN TO SAY "NO"?

Be honest.

Most of the time we say "Yes" to everything because we don't want to let the other person down or make them feel bad.

And then we complicate the issue when we try and make up excuses about why we can't do something.

But just be honest.

When you are honest, you will respond with respect. I guarantee you will also then receive respect for your decision. People may not like it, and there will always be those who want to force their agenda on you no matter what, but they will have to respect you for your decision to say, "No, thank you."

You may feel that honesty is not always the best policy. Sure, when your wife or girlfriend asks, "Do I look good in this dress?" that's a good time to go and practice your putting.

But being very clear and realistic about what you can handle is vital if you want to stay sane in this world.

I travel a ridiculous amount and am surrounded by people. I have incredible levels of energy and am blessed with this. But there is a point where I do have to say "No" to certain things.

I cannot always control how the other person will react. Quite frankly, that's also not my job. They are as much in charge of their emotions and lives as I am in charge of mine. But by being honest I know that I am not putting all of us in a possibly even worse situation by committing to something on which I cannot follow through.

There is no shame in knowing your limits, and we all have limits. You just cannot be everything to everybody, no matter how good your intentions are.

Knowing your limits and managing your schedule effectively is critically important. That's how you get the best work done. Not *ALL OF THE WORK*, but the best work.

On a golf course, if your caddie says, "Hit it over that water hazard" and you know for a fact you don't have the distance or ability to do that, are you going to do it in any case just to please him? Of course not. That's what knowing your limits is about. There are certain things I could never do and can still not do on a golf course. Did it limit my career or success? I don't think so. I understood them and worked to my strengths. If we could all say "Yes" to everything and get it all done, well, what would be the need for so many individuals in this world? The whole point is that there are things you can do that others can't, and there are things you cannot do. There is absolutely no shame whatsoever in knowing what these are. On the contrary, this knowledge will make you a better and more effective human being.

So be honest. Don't be wishy-washy. Be sincere and respectful in your reply. Saying a delicate "No" with poise and respect is the secret.

And again, I cannot emphasize enough that the other person may not be entirely happy with your response, but they cannot argue that you have given them a thoughtful and considered opinion.

14. HOW DO YOU NOT GET SUCKED INTO THE PESSIMISM OF THOSE AROUND YOU?

I love the story in the Bible of David and Goliath. Not for the obvious lesson that it teaches, but for a point made by somebody I once heard preaching on the topic.

He said that the Israelite army saw Goliath as too big to hit. But David saw Goliath as too big to miss.

Isn't that a wonderful way of conveying exactly the difference between a pessimist and an optimist?

David was an optimist not because he just blindly believed everything would turn out okay. He still had to face his own fear of what was a giant of a man. He still had to overcome the taunts and insults of the soldiers around him. He still had to overcome the pessimism of his own brothers as to whether he was up to the task.

But his different point of view made him an optimist in the best sense of the word.

That's what I try and bring to every challenge I face—a different perspective.

I'm so glad you used the words "sucked into" in your question. That's exactly what pessimism is. It's like quicksand or a black hole. Simply being close to it is bad for you, and it will suck you in before you know it.

So to start off, I counter pessimism by not being around pessimistic people.

The negativity of certain people astounds me. I don't know how some people can go through life being so negative. I avoid them like I avoid bacon.

I once saw a movie about a young artist who was training with a master. When the young artist asked the master why he always painted beautiful pictures, the master replied, "Because any old idiot can paint what's wrong with the world."

I feel the same way about pessimism.

Any old idiot can see what's wrong with the world. That doesn't take a genius to figure out. Let's face it, every single one of us could wake up each morning with a long list of complaints. And many of them would be valid. We'd be justified in our complaining. But where does that get us?

As I've said so many times, optimism is not some head-in-the-sand philosophy that looks at life through rose-colored glasses and says everything is fine despite the obvious hardships and challenges out there.

Optimism and a positive attitude will enable you to see the obstacles and challenges, to accept the hardships and suffering, but to always be open to finding a way through it.

15. HOW DO YOU DEAL WITH ANGER AND RESENTMENT?

The first time I met Nelson Mandela was shortly after his release from Robben Island and prison on February 11, 1990.

I asked him how he could have no hatred or revenge in his heart. He said, "Gary, I love people, even those who put me in jail. I want to bring my 50 million children in this country together. You've got to live with love, Gary."

People such as Mandela, Mother Theresa, Ghandi, Martin Luther King—they are the ones who go down in history as the greats because they all had such love for their fellow man. It is through people such as these that I learned early on in my life and my career that hatred and jealousy are two of the worst things in life.

Mandela said to me, "Gary, we've all got to learn to work together and play our part."

What Nelson Mandela taught all of us about anger and resentment is the power of forgiveness.

Learn to forgive.

Mandela was imprisoned for 27 years. His best years were spent breaking rocks in a quarry on Robben Island.

But as he showed all of us, the true power of forgiveness lies not in the person being forgiven, but in the person doing the forgiving.

There is much that hurts us deeply in the world, not least of which is the actions of others.

But when you carry this around with you, you are the loser. It will eat you up and destroy you.

You can't move forward in life with this baggage of anger and resentment on your back.

Forgive, and feel the freedom it brings.

Love is such a powerful force. Show a bit of love to yourself by letting go of the anger and resentment that is dragging you down.

Forgive whoever has hurt you, and get on with living your own life.

16. I AM TRYING TO TEACH MY CHILDREN HOW TO DEAL WITH FAILURE IN A POSITIVE WAY. ANY ADVICE?

Do you know what the most incredible Major record in golf is?

Not the 18 Majors Jack Nicklaus won. It was the 19 in which he finished second.

That is the most runner-up finishes by any golfer in the history of the Majors.

So not only does Jack have the most wins ever in Major history as a record. He also holds the record for having just lost in Majors.

He is the best golfer in Major championship history. And he is also the best loser in Major championship history. He is the most gracious in defeat of any I played against.

I say this with the utmost respect for my great friend Jack, because he has taught me so much about seeing such things in the right light.

Teach your children how to fail like that, and you will have done your job well.

In 1988, I was playing some of my best golf on the senior tour. I went into the US Senior Open at Medinah Country Club that year supremely confident. I opened with a 74. In my best year, I shot my worst round.

That 74 shook me to my core. I managed to hang in there, though, and I just had to grind my way through that Major.

In the final round, Bob Charles was three shots clear of me with four holes to play. He bogeyed the next three holes. I kept on grinding away and making pars, hardly feeling like I was playing winning golf in any way.

Bob and I were tied for the lead playing the 18th and we both made par to force a playoff. In the playoff I shot a 68 to his 70.

It felt a bit like I'd been "failing" for four rounds in that Major, and then suddenly I made the breakthrough.

It's important to let your children know that failure is a fact of life. They are going to fail, several times at several things.

They need to know that it's perfectly normal to fail to win, but not to fail to learn.

It's a common fact in professional sports that we learn more from our defeats than we do from our victories.

I know I always came away with greater enlightenment and a sense of growth when I had failed than when I won.

Teach your children that failure is not the end but merely a part of their overall journey to success in something.

It's not a question of teaching them to accept failure and become mediocre. It's more about them learning to use failure as the step up to becoming better.

It's a lot like physical training.

When you train your muscles, the process of overloading them or stressing your body is vital to helping it get stronger.

Physical training is in essence a controlled process of putting your body under stress and breaking it down so that it can rebuild itself into an even stronger version.

That's exactly how your children should learn to view failure—as part of the process designed to make you better.

Otherwise, how would we grow? How would we improve ourselves if we didn't see where we are going wrong?

You don't know you're doing something wrong in your golf swing until you hit it sideways. That's when you can begin the process of correcting it.

Don't get them to see failure as a friend. You don't want your children to become comfortable with failure. The top sportsmen are certainly not comfortable with failure. They hate it as much as the next person. But they know how to use it.

So your job is to help your children see that failure is like a mentor to them. A mentor doesn't tell you what you want to hear. A good mentor who is interested in your growth as a human being tells you what you *need* to hear.

Failure is that mentor.

17. HOW DO YOU KNOW WHEN TO KEEP PUSHING FORWARD NO MATTER THE OBSTACLES THAT ARE IN YOUR WAY, OR WHEN IT'S TIME TO QUIT AND MOVE ON TO SOMETHING ELSE?

Golfers will often say that the pressure of being in the hunt and chasing down a tournament win is the reason we practice. To an extent that's true. But that pressure doesn't come without a price.

In 1962 and 1973, it very nearly killed my love for the game. There were two Majors where it was particularly bad.

In the 1962 Masters, I was involved in a playoff for the title with Arnold Palmer and Dow Finsterwald. I was defending the title I had won a year before, when I beat Arnold on his home turf. And yet, it was the last place I wanted to be that day.

I woke up that morning and I had this mental block about going to the golf course. I just couldn't face it. I felt weak just thinking about the people, the press, and everything that goes with The Masters. I looked at my hands, and they were quite literally shaking. Eventually I managed to get myself into a car and to Augusta National Golf Club. But still I wasn't myself. I stepped onto the first tee as the defending champion. Huge galleries had already lined the fairway on either side. But I felt utterly alone and insignificant. I started well, with two straight birdies. Dow fell out early on, and it was really just Arnold and me on the back nine. Arnold eventually shot 68 while I carded a 71. I was not happy.

Then in 1973, I arrived at Troon for the British Open. Again it hit me: Is this what I want to keep doing with my life? I would say this was perhaps the biggest crisis of confidence I have ever suffered in my career. It was like I'd suddenly snapped out of the dream of becoming a world champion, and I'd reached a point where I was close to hating the game.

The very thing that had given me all my success, all the money to buy my beloved horses and my farm in Colesberg, all the security to provide for my family—this same thing was now keeping me away from it all. I was on an endless treadmill of travel, time changes, dinner parties, talks, media interviews, and everything that goes with success at the highest level of golf. And I had begun to resent it.

At Troon I kept telling myself that I had the willpower to snap out of my funk and dig deep as I had done so many times before—to battle through it. I never spoke to anybody about it. Only Vivienne knew about my inner turmoil. But I know Jack Nicklaus had the same feelings. He reached a point where he suddenly succumbed to self-doubt. "Tell me, am I really finished?" he once asked his wife Barbara.

In 1973, I reached a similar low point—easily the lowest of my career. I seriously considered packing it all in and walking away from everything before I was even 40. One night, I looked at Vivienne and said words I never thought would come out of my mouth. "I feel like quitting," I told her. I poured out my heart to her, and she just listened. At the end of it all she said, "The decision is yours. Whatever you decide, I will support you."

I went through the motions at Troon. Then I went home to my farm in South Africa. And it was there that I found something again. I worked on a change to my swing, but I also did what I love to do on my farm, and that's get my hands dirty and sweat a little. It was like a cleansing moment. And then it was back. The desire to win, the passion, and the drive to succeed all came flooding back to me. And a year later I had one of my best seasons, winning two Majors in The Masters and the British Open as well as eight other victories worldwide.

But that's what Major Championship golf can do to a man. It can take you to unbelievable highs, but just as quickly bring you right down to the pit of despair.

I've always only known one thing, and that's to never give up.

I was taught this lesson early in my life by my brother Ian, and I've never forgotten it.

It is now so ingrained in my personality. Never, never, never give up.

But I agree that you need to be realistic, as well.

I had made a decision that what I lacked in natural talent I would make up for in hard work. In other words, I needed to develop a culture of determination and perseverance in order to achieve my goal.

They were my enablers for where I felt I was lacking in other areas. But they never replaced common sense.

Yes, once I had decided on something, I would go at it with everything I had and push through any challenges to get there. But it was a strategic approach to my goals. I was never silly about the process. Einstein once said the definition of insanity is doing the same thing over and over and expecting a different result. Well, I was never insane.

You will know when to keep pushing forward when you know how important this goal is to you, and how much you have thought through the process. That is when you develop real determination and perseverance. Anybody can just blindly crash forward in the hope that something is going to change, but the truly determined ones are clever enough to know how to push forward. Sometimes "forward" may be going backwards a few steps, or sideways to find another way.

It's like playing links golf. Finding yourself in a deep pot bunker is a fact of links golf. It's going to happen at some point in your round. Determination is knowing your ultimate goal of winning a links tournament, and realizing that you may have to chip out sideways or backwards of a pot bunker to get there.

Silly is, despite being in a pot bunker, trying to keep hitting the ball forward and hitting the face of the bunker all the time.

I don't care if you do that till your hands bleed and you feel pretty proud of your perseverance; I think you'd agree that it's a silly approach.

Be honest with yourself about the challenges when they come. Ask yourself—are they are an obstacle to be overcome, or a sign that you are now starting to get silly?

18. I HAVE BEEN HURT VERY BADLY BY PEOPLE I TRUSTED, OR WHO I THOUGHT RESPECTED ME. HOW DO YOU FORGIVE THOSE WHO HURT YOU?

Individuals will let you down, and people will hurt you.

But you cannot let it affect your faith in all of humanity.

You forgive just by making a decision to do so. Just do it, and do it with love. Don't overthink it. Don't delay. Don't put any conditions to your forgiveness. Just forgive and feel the weight lift off your own shoulders.

I've been hurt deeply by situations. One of the most hurtful involved my friend Nelson Mandela.

In September 2007, a journalist from the *Guardian* newspaper in England correctly identified that I had designed a golf course in Burma (also known as Myanmar). The journalist then tied this to my association with the Nelson Mandela Invitational in South Africa. This was a tournament conceived by myself and my son Marc. The idea was that I would use my profile to help bring leading golfers, celebrities, and businessmen together in

a tournament that raised millions of rands for the Nelson Mandela Children's Fund. Fifty percent of the funds would go to the Nelson Mandela Children's Fund, and fifty percent to the Gary Player Foundation. Over the years, I am extremely proud of the fact that we raised millions upon millions of rands for so many underprivileged children.

The journalist asked how Nelson Mandela could align himself with someone who invested in a golf course in Burma that was displacing a village and with its human rights violations there. It mattered not that neither of these accusations was true. This journalist then proceeded to quote, completely out of context, from one of my earlier books—*Grand Slam Golf*—in which I stated how proud I was to be a South African. The insinuation was that my pride for my country somehow meant I "supported" apartheid and was now "supporting" similar oppression in Burma through my golf course design activities there.

Yes, we did build a design course in Burma. But at the time we built it, the political situation there was a lot more optimistic than it later became. It looked like there was real potential for change, and I have always believed in the power of golf to help bring about social change. It created local jobs and helped tourism.

This article filtered back to South Africa, and Archbishop Desmond Tutu was asked to give his opinion as the head of the Save Burma campaign. I respect Tutu immensely and believe I can call him a friend. But I don't think he had all the facts when asked for a quote. Tutu said that if this was all true, then Mandela shouldn't be involved with the Nelson Mandela Invitational any longer, and by association with Gary Player.

That hurt.

A week later the Nelson Mandela Children's Fund asked us for an official response, which we sent through to them. Then they issued their own statement saying that I should relinquish my involvement with the Nelson Mandela Invitational.

Needless to say, it was one of the worst periods of my life. I was attacked in the media, and ultimately we agreed to terminating the use of the Mandela name and changed it to the Gary Player Invitational. The result is that all of the good this tournament had achieved had come to an end, and with it the support for the underprivileged children it helped.

I received a lot of support during the incident, for which I am grateful. But I also received a lot of criticism, and much of it from people I believe were not properly informed but did not care to hear the truth. And I know that my friend Nelson Mandela was not happy with what happened, and he told me as much. He also made a public statement, which Tutu supported, as well, that the event should go on but the damage had been done and our relationship with the Children's Fund was beyond repair.

One of my most cherished memories is of welcoming Mandela to one of our Nelson Mandela Invitational tournaments before the above controversy took place. He arrived in a helicopter and landed at the Pecanwood Golf and Country Club outside Pretoria. I walked up to the door of the helicopter, and as he stepped out he held open his arms and said, "Gary, do you still remember me?" How could you forget the most recognizable man on the planet? But such was his humility. And such was his love for people.

There will always be those who criticize, those who sit on the sidelines and say, "You could have done more." And I have never sought a pat on the back for anything I have done. Yes, it hurts me that when my country makes history by hosting the FIFA World Cup in 2010 and I am at the stadium for the opening ceremony, I didn't receive an invite from my own president to visit him in his suite. I have been hurt by how little recognition I have received from my government.

But Mandela taught me to see beyond these things, just as he did. He looked beyond the hurt and saw the bigger picture of what he wanted to achieve for his country. He forgave, so that he—and in turn all of us—could move forward.

People have criticized me throughout my career.

But at that meeting with Mandela, he said to me, "Gary, thank you for being such a great ambassador for our country."

We have no option but to forgive if we have any hope of moving forward in life.

Forgive, and love. Then, as the world's greatest prisoner showed us all, you will truly be free.

19. HOW DO YOU STRIKE A BALANCE BETWEEN PRIDE AND HUMILITY?

At the 1974 Open Championship at Royal Lytham, I came as close as I think I have ever come to golf perfection.

I played my best golf that week. I was five strokes ahead of the field after 36 holes. With two holes to play, I was six shots ahead of the field.

I was just in such control of my game that week. I felt invincible on the golf course, and it showed as I went on to win my third Open Championship in as many decades.

You can start to feel pretty good about yourself when you reach those kinds of milestones.

But as perfect as my game was at that moment, I felt I was more confident than arrogant.

You can be confident without being arrogant. There is a humility about true confidence. A humility to say, "I'm going to

work as hard as I can and put everything into this," which in turn breeds the confidence to achieve.

Arrogance lacks this very important foundation. Arrogance says, "I'm great just because I am." Confidence says, "I'm great because I've worked so hard to become who I am."

There is a fine line between confidence and arrogance. And beware, jealous people will always have their own interpretations of this.

Arrogance is self-centeredness, and when you are self-centered there is no room for growth. Confidence is a belief in your own ability without a belief in the inferiority of others.

20. I AM VERY BAD AT HANDLING STRESS. IT STARTS TO AFFECT ME PHYSICALLY. HOW DID YOU HANDLE STRESSFUL MOMENTS IN YOUR LIFE?

There was a time at a tournament in Durban when I felt the pressure on me was becoming unbearable. My brother Ian and I were in a hotel elevator, and I just broke down and told Ian that I couldn't handle it anymore. He spoke to me calmly and clearly and, as always, convinced me that I could.

Stress is one of the "diseases" of our modern age.

I read recently of a study done in America that found 46 percent of employees felt greater stress from their workload than even the stress of job security.

Another study conducted in 2014 found that 77 percent of Americans regularly experience physical symptoms caused by stress. This includes fatigue, headaches, upset stomachs, and even dizziness.

It's a mess.

I keep hammering on about exercise and correct nutrition because it's a fact that people who are overweight or obese are more likely to experience stress. This is particularly true in over-weight or obese children, who in a 2010 stress study in America revealed that they worry and stress more than healthy children their age.

The impact a parent's health decisions have on a child are immense. It's also been found that parents who are obese are more likely to have children who are overweight.

So it's vital to start here. Regular exercise and correct nutrition play a major part in helping to combat the negative effects—physical and mental—of stress.

You need to take these precautions because nobody is immune to stress.

The mental effects of stress are hard enough to deal with that you don't need to complicate the matter by bringing on the physical effects thereof as well through bad lifestyle choices.

As a society we consume so much caffeine in various drinks in our day, yet it's been found that this actually amplifies stress. It becomes a vicious cycle that we keep feeding.

I don't drink a lot of coffee. I don't drink any caffeinated cold drinks or fizzy drinks. So I would start managing your stress by beginning with your health and fitness.

If you don't already exercise, then get busy. All studies suggest that there is a positive connection between exercise and the management of the physical and mental effects of stress. One study found that as few as five minutes of exercise can help to reduce feelings of anxiety. Five minutes! It takes longer to make and drink a cup of coffee.

And listen to this. What is the one thing that helps astronauts counter the stress on the body of being weightless in space? Exercise. So much so that astronauts on the International Space Station are forced to exercise two hours a day.

Start by making a lifestyle change if you need to, and I guarantee this will have an impact on how you handle stress.

Then I would suggest that you find other areas in your life that help to calm you, and tap into these.

In 1964 my brother Ian and I had one of the most memorable trips of my life.

Ian had just been appointed Chief Conservator for Zululand in what is now the KwaZulu-Natal province of South Africa. I had already won three Majors. I suppose you could say we were both at the pinnacle of our chosen professions. Yet on that trip we came together just as brothers again. We camped in a hut on the beach, and we fished from early morning to late night. We gathered wood from the nearby dune forest and cooked our fish over the coals. We told stories, swam in the sea, and enjoyed absolute freedom. It was such a relief for me to feel so free when there were already great demands on my time. It was one of the few moments in what had become my very crowded life when I was away from hundreds of people, telephones, television, radio, and the media.

We went back to being just the two brothers who used to jump into puddles after thunderstorms and challenge each other in feats of strength and endurance.

I needed moments like that just to center me again. Find these opportunities in life, and share them with the people you know are a calming influence on you.

I've needed to find these moments of calm at various times in my career.

21. WHAT IS YOUR DEFINITION OF SUCCESS IN LIFE?

I consider my greatest success in life as being able to help my fellow human beings.

I always wanted to be a champion golfer, but there was also a strong desire in me to use that status and success to help people.

That desire was there when I handed over my winner's check from the 1965 US Open to the United States Golf Association and asked them to donate to cancer research and to junior golf development.

I don't think that that desire to help people has ever really left me. I can't think of anything worse than a child who is suffering. I always said that when I'm successful I'm going to just help some children have some sweetness in their life. I lead a privileged life, so I see it as my duty to give back to people who don't have those opportunities. We formed The Player Foundation more than 30 years ago, and in this time have raised more than $62 million for underprivileged children on six continents. We have our Gary Player Invitational tournaments in Europe, North America, Asia, South Africa, and the Middle East and they raise a phenomenal amount for charity every year. They do so with the help of all our friends in the golf, business, and entertainment industries. I want to look back on my life and say I've contributed more than just golf to this world. I want to be remembered more as a good human being than a great golfer.

I once visited a school for settlement-area children in Cape Town, South Africa, and it left an indelible imprint on my mind. I rank that day as one of the top five days of my life. When we visited this school, the children received me so warmly. They sang a song for me, and many of them knew all about my career, which surprised me. I was so choked up by the fact that

these kids had never slept between two white sheets, never sat on a proper toilet or in a proper bath, never gone to school in a car. But they still had this amazing optimism. They were so happy.

I felt so encouraged that our country could produce these children under such difficult circumstances. When I left, the kids hugged me and wouldn't let go. I got in the car and cried like a baby. To be able to raise money for people who need it—that's very special. On my farm in South Africa I have built a small church and school, and we host an annual sports day for the local children.

And then you have moments where you realize the difference you have made in someone's life. In 2007, I was walking in the Cape Town city center and I heard somebody call my name. I looked behind me and there was nobody. Then I heard it again. After a while I looked up, and a young black man was leaning out of an office window. He shouted down at me, "Thank you, Gary. I've got this great job because of the education you gave me."

You never forget moments like that, just as you never forget struggling.

True success is judged by your relationship with your fellow human beings. This life is about making a difference. It's not about personal enrichment or glory. Someone once said that we are blessed so that we can be a blessing to others.

To simply garner success for yourself can become a very unrewarding experience. Your success needs to positively impact others for it to have wide-ranging benefits for society as a whole.

We've had some wonderful moments raising money around the world. I remember one charity visit we did to a village in rural KwaZulu-Natal in South Africa. The village was on this muddy slope deep in a sugar cane field. We were visiting a community project where the ladies of the village collect waste, take it to a central point, and then earn points with which they can "buy" small trees. They plant these trees, and when they've reached a certain number, they receive a bicycle. South African soccer legend Lucas Radebe was with me, and we were going to hand over a few of these bicycles. A bicycle is one of the most important things in rural Africa because it can help an entire family, from transporting a child to school far away from the village to fetching water. One of the features of the bicycles is that they have a rack for luggage on the back, which I told the ladies was "perfect for my mother-in-law."

As we were handing out these bicycles, I decided to climb on one and do my balancing trick. The ladies loved it. It was such a heartwarming moment. What I love about African women is that they can always laugh with you, no matter how desperate their situation is. I even got a giggle out of them when I asked if they knew what the cricket score was. It was the second day of the first cricket Test between South Africa and Australia. When I was given an update of the ridiculous carnage that was unfolding as South Africa were being bundled out, I said, "Man, I stayed on the bike for longer than that." They didn't know much about cricket, but man, did they have a good laugh about that.

I suppose at the end of everything I've done, I would like to look back and say I've contributed more than just good golf to this world.

I want to be remembered not as a great athlete but someone who did everything in his power to make life better and contribute to the well-being of my fellow man.

Our world faces so many challenges today, and into this we bring a spirit of giving and the knowledge that we can do something to make a difference.

What I would like written on my tombstone one day is the following: "He loved his fellow human beings."

PART II

THE
QUESTIONS
OF GOLF

I've been a golf professional for 64 years.

I've won 167 tournaments everywhere from America and Europe to Brazil, Chile, Japan, Egypt, Australia, and of course South Africa.

I've won on the regular tours. I've won on the senior tours.

I've won nine Majors on the regular tour and nine on the PGA Champions Tour.

I've won tournaments in multiple decades, including becoming the first non-American to win the Grand Slam.

I've learned from Ben Hogan, Bobby Locke, Sam Snead, and so many other great golfers.

I've studied this game for more than 60 years, with the result that I know a heck of a lot about nothing.

When it comes to the golf swing, I've seen it all.

I've played the impossible shots. I mean, let's be honest, how impossible is a hole-in-one?

I've had 31 holes-in-one during tournaments in my life, the most recent of which was on the seventh during the 2016 Masters Par 3 Contest at Augusta National. That made me the oldest to achieve this, at the age of 80. I had my first hole-in-one when I was 15 years old.

Let me tell you, I've seen it all when it comes to this side of the game. I had a hole-in-one on four holes on four different golf courses—twice.

I'll never forget the look on the faces of Arnold Palmer and Jack Nicklaus when we played together in The Tradition tournament on the Champions Tour at Desert Mountain in Arizona.

We reached the par-three seventh hole, which has a double green shared with the 15th hole. I hit a 6 iron and it went straight into the hole. When we reached that green again, playing it as the par-five 15th, I holed a wedge for eagle. They couldn't believe I'd just had an ace and an eagle on the same green in the same round.

I once won a tournament thanks to a hole-in-one. It was in New Zealand. I was playing a match play event against David Thomas. I was five down, and then we reached this par four that had a narrow pathway between the bunkers leading to the green.

My tee shot somehow landed on this and kicked and rolled all the way onto the green and in the hole. A hole-in-one on a par four. Can you believe it? Well, Thomas couldn't. It shook him up so much I ended up beating him.

Then you consider that Ben Hogan, the straightest hitter the world ever knew, only had one hole-in-one in his career. And my father, who played golf for 40 years, never had one.

Then take my wife, Vivienne. She once had two holes-in-one in the same round of golf at Johannesburg's Wanderers Golf Club in 1978. And the crazy thing is that she could've had a third that day. Her tee shot on another par three stopped centimeters short of the hole.

She phoned me where I was overseas at the time playing in a tournament and said, "Beat that!"

Editor's Note: *The right/left designations in this section are specific to right-handed golfers. Left-handed golfers should make adjustments accordingly.*

1. SOMETIMES, OUT OF NOWHERE, I'LL DEVELOP A SLICE OR A HOOK THAT FOR THE LIFE OF ME I CANNOT STOP. I DON'T KNOW WHETHER IT'S A CONCENTRATION ISSUE, BUT IT COSTS ME VALUABLE SHOTS DURING MY ROUND. IS THERE A QUICK FIX FOR WHEN THIS STARTS HAPPENING DURING MY ROUND?

Let me start by saying I'm not Houdini or a great magician who can just suddenly make you stop hooking or slicing a golf ball. Even the very best professionals have the occasional hook or slice out of nowhere.

A hook or a slice/fade can be either created or corrected by a change of the grip.

If you're hooking the golf ball and you want to fade it, then make your grip weaker. If you're a right-handed golfer, to make your grip weaker move your hands more to the left.

If you're fading the ball and you want to hook it, then strengthen your grip. Again, if you're a right-handed golfer, you do this by moving your hands more to the right. I would recommend for most amateurs that they aim to see three knuckles on their left hand as an indication of the grip being correct. As you get better and closer to scratch, seeing two knuckles would be the grip I recommend.

If you find yourself slicing the ball, you could also try to just relax your left hand and grip a bit more tightly with your right.

And if you are hooking the ball and want to get back to hitting it straight, then try relaxing your right hand and gripping the club more tightly with your left. I call it strangling the hook by strangling the club with your left hand.

Also, remember to not lose control of your grip at the top of your backswing. Many amateurs suffer from this problem, namely, opening their hands at the top of their backswing. If you do this you lose all the power in your swing, and control of the club.

Your hands must remain firm throughout the swing. Another tip for this would be to make sure that the life line in your right palm covers your left thumb when you grip the club.

You could also just put your hands together and then, without twisting them, slide them down and over the club and then grip it.

Or you could put a leaf between the palms of your hand and then grip the club, trying not to let it drop out when you swing.

The above advice would be the best way to try and correct a hook or slice when playing under pressure. But you've got to remember that there is no quick fix in this game.

There's no magic wand you can just wave and presto, problem solved.

You've got to practice.

I could give you at least 10 things you should do to stop hooking or slicing the golf ball, but they would require tremendous practice.

I would also tell you that although these fixes can help, when you stop hooking or slicing the ball I'd want you to get back to your normal grip as soon as possible.

And remember, go see a pro. It might cost you a little dough, but he's in the know.

2. I ALWAYS SEEM TO TENSE UP WHENEVER I GET TO MY BALL AND SEE IT'S IN A BAD LIE. IT'S AS IF I'M ALREADY EXPECTING A BAD RESULT. WHAT DO YOU DO WHEN YOU'RE FACED WITH A BAD LIE?

You're no different from anybody else in this game, my friend. We all do that. It's part of golf.

My advice is quite simple: don't cry, but don't reach for the sky, either.

When faced with a bad lie in the rough, just be focused on getting the ball back onto the fairway.

Take your punishment like a man, or a woman.

Remember, you're not the only one on the golf course getting bad lies.

Yes, there are certain things you need to consider when playing a shot from a bad lie.

You mentioned how you tense up. Well, this is a perfectly natural physical response, and you need to counter it.

When you tense up, you will grip the club too tightly. Your whole body will be too tight and it will probably see you duff your shot.

So when you address your ball, make a conscious effort to relax your shoulders and your body.

Bend your knees and feel relaxed.

You may want to take your club back a bit slower on the your backswing, and then whip it through as you normally would.

Take an extra club if you feel you need it to counter the bad lie.

But the best advice I can give is to get out of trouble. Don't try and be greedy. Take your medicine, get your ball back on the fairway, and then go from there.

But also remember that the greatest players in the game have all endured bad lies. And bad weather.

The two best bad-weather players I ever saw were Tom Watson and Arnold Palmer. The worse the conditions got, the better they played.

See that bad lie as a challenge to bring out your best golf.

3. I WAS ONE STROKE AHEAD OF MY OPPONENT, AND ALL I NEEDED ON THE LAST HOLE TO WIN WAS A PAR. I ENDED UP MAKING DOUBLE BOGEY AND LOST. WHAT DID I DO WRONG?

Well, I'm gong to be as kind as I can here, but you did everything wrong.

First of all, you started by saying "*ALL* I need is a par to win." Are you Tiger Woods? How good are you?

I can tell you, even Tiger Woods struggled to make a par when he needed a par to win.

So it's not *ALL* you need.

If you're not Tiger Woods and are a weekend golfer like most people, then you should be thinking of taking the pressure off yourself and playing for a bogey that will get you into a playoff.

If you make par, then it's a bonus.

It's a whole different philosophy.

When in the heat of competition, never allow yourself to think along the lines of "ALL I need . . ." It dulls your focus, even if for only a second. You need to remain alert at all times and be able to consider every eventuality.

If you can give yourself an extra shot and still be in the hunt for the win, then do so.

By forcing yourself to make this par, you'll end up trying to steer the ball off the tee in the hope that you don't make a mistake, and the result will be a forced shot that puts you in trouble.

Now you're on the back foot off the tee, you try and go for the big shot with your second and put yourself into even more trouble, and as you say you end up making a six when even a bogey would've kept you in the competition.

How many times have you seen a professional play for the middle of the green to give himself a comfortable two putts to maybe make a playoff or win a tournament? I can tell you, my bank manager never asked me how I won.

Think of it this way: if you needed to make birdie on the last to beat your opponent, would you be standing on the tee saying to yourself, "I have to make a birdie?"

If you're like most weekend golfers, you wouldn't.

You'd tell yourself that you're going to do your best on the last hole, and if you make a birdie it's a bonus.

So why shift the goalposts and make it that much harder for yourself?

Be realistic, use all the shots you are given, and take the pressure off yourself.

Golf is about thinking clever, not thinking like a hero.

4. HOW DO I GET MORE POWER IN MY LONG GAME WITHOUT BUYING BETTER CLUBS?

With a little thing called exercise. And flexibility.

To hit it farther you need to get stronger, and more supple.

So I would start by getting more in shape in the gym.

From a technical point of view, you've got to learn to rotate your hips when you come into the ball. Most of your power comes from your hips, not your arms. Your glutes are some of the strongest muscles in your body, far stronger than your biceps.

A wide backswing and a wide extension on your follow-through are also key to hitting the ball farther.

A technique I used when I felt my follow-through was a bit too short was to take a club and swing it through some long grass, without a ball.

The grass offers great resistance, so it forces you to really concentrate on swinging through. I would do this for a few minutes in practice just to get that feel back of swinging through and developing that wide extension again.

I've also seen so many amateurs get ready to hit it long and then you can see how they tense up, grip the club tighter, and are using all of their power on the backswing already.

Great golfers don't hit the ball farther by making themselves hit it harder. They have an even smoother swing that saves all the power for when it matters—when hitting through the ball.

Get those hips, legs, and shoulders working through the ball.

Another thing that might be taking the power out of your shot is that you are falling back on the shot. It's a common mistake made by many weekend golfers.

Here you need to focus on your right knee (if you are a right-handed golfer) and getting it to bend into the shot when you play. If you watch my swing you'll see I always tuck that right knee in before I start with my backswing. It makes the right side of my body more relaxed and helps me transfer my weight through the ball and onto the left foot.

Balance will also be key in generating power.

Cock your head slightly to the right before you swing, and as you swing stay with the ball by feeling as if your head were going in the opposite direction from your hands. A steady head helps tremendously with your balance.

If you want to work on your balance, do what I used to do.

I would often go out in to the garden with just a five iron in my hands and wearing a normal pair of shoes, and then swing the club a few times.

My aim wasn't to try and swing hard, but to remind myself to work on my balance. Without wearing golf shoes, you don't have the grip, so you need to consciously work on your balance. It's a great routine that I would highly recommend.

5. I SOMETIMES STRUGGLE TO FEEL COMFORTABLE IN MY STANCE, AND I OFTEN END UP STANDING EITHER TOO CLOSE OR TOO FAR FROM THE BALL. IS THERE A SHORT CHECKLIST I CAN DO TO MAKE SURE I'M THE CORRECT DISTANCE FROM MY BALL?

Yes there is.

Make sure your left arm is extended with the club and your right elbow touches your hip. Then you'll know you'll be the same distance from the ball every time.

6. HOW SHOULD I ADJUST MY SWING FOR PLAYING IN THE WIND?

Very simple. When it's breezy, you swing easy.

The minute you start trying to hit hard in the wind, you're gone.

Also, there is no such thing as trying to hit the ball low. Let me explain.

If you've got a wedge to the green and you take a 7 iron and grip down on the shaft and hit it soft, the ball goes low by itself and you have it under control.

Trying to hit a hard wedge into the wind will balloon the ball, and you'll probably never find it.

Remember this—in the wind, hit it high and you'll cry. Hit it low and you'll make the dough.

7. WHENEVER MY BALL IS ON SOFT, MARSHY GROUND, I ALWAYS END UP TAKING A HUGE DIVOT AND THE BALL GOES NOWHERE. HOW DO I CHANGE THIS?

First of all, when you have that kind of lie, if you've got a 9 iron to the green, take an 8 iron and grip it shorter.

The next tip involves your stance.

Whenever I found myself on that kind of wet or marshy ground, I would position the ball more toward my left foot.

The rationale behind this is that from this kind of lie you want to be hitting the ball on the upswing. If the ball is positioned too far back in your stance you run the risk of taking a divot, which from the fairway is fine, but from such a soggy lie will kill your power and the ball will go nowhere.

The next thing I do is make sure that I hit the ball clean. I don't want to hit down on the ball in this instance. I want to hit the top of the ball. So I keep my focus on the top of the ball. In this way my club hits the ball first and not the marshy ground.

I often feel in these conditions it's far better to hit the ball thin than fat.

A simple thought for you with a lie like this would be "Thin to win. Fat and you're still on that mat of soggy ground."

8. HOW DO I PLAY A BUNKER SHOT FROM A PLUGGED LIE?

I love bunker shots, probably because I have practiced them so much over the years.

It was from practicing bunker shots that my famous saying became so popular.

It was in Texas in 1958. I was practicing a bunker shot, and a man stopped to watch me. I holed the first shot he saw. So he said, "You've got 50 bucks if you hole the next one." I took the bet and holed it. Then he upped it to $100 if I could do it again. And I did it—three times in a row. As he handed me the money he said, "Son, I've never seen anyone so lucky in my life."

"Well, Sir," I said, "The harder I practice, the luckier I get."

My wife Vivienne remembers how when we were still dating I would tell her that I'd pick her up at a certain time after I was done practicing.

Then I'd start practicing bunker shots, and I was determined not to leave until I had holed 10 of them.

Poor Vivienne knew that if I was late it was because I still hadn't holed those 10 bunker shots yet.

I would also always practice bad lies in a bunker. I'd give myself uneven lies—uphill, downhill, and yes, plugged lies. My reasoning was that I'd become so good at playing bad lies in a bunker that if I was presented with a good lie in a bunker, it would make me feel really confident.

Confidence is a major factor in successful golf.

When it comes to a plugged lie in a bunker, the first thing you need to do is keep the ball in the middle of your stance.

Stand wide, cock your wrists on the backswing as quick as you can, keep the clubface square at address and not open, and hit down an inch behind the ball. Also, don't follow through. And whatever you do, never try and scoop the ball out of the sand.

All of this will make the ball pop up out of that lie. But you need to remember that when it hits the green it will have no backspin.

It's impossible to generate backspin on this kind of shot. So you need to allow for the extra run on the green.

If you want to try and stop the ball quickly on the green from this kind of shot, then you're going to have to blast it out really high to counter that extra run. But that would mean breaking your wrists very quickly on the backswing and coming down really steep into the sand. It requires a lot of practice and confidence to tackle this kind of shot, so I would rather you just allow for getting your ball out and onto the green and accept that you'll get a little bit of extra run.

The only way you can really get the feel for this kind of shot is to practice, practice, practice.

9. I OFTEN END UP THINNING MY CHIP SHOTS FROM HARD GROUND. HOW DO YOU PLAY THESE DELICATE SHOTS OFF HARD SURFACES?

Everybody makes this mistake.

If you are faced with a hard lie around the green, don't be scared to use that putter.

And please don't use your sand wedge. Rather, take your 7 iron and run the ball up. Or take your rescue club and it will rescue your shot if you play it like a putter.

I know of so many professionals who do that.

My advice would be to stay away from wedges around the greens unless you have to go over something, such as a bunker or something else.

A wedge played off a bare lie is almost always going to see you hit too far behind the ball, which means the clubface will bounce off the bare ground and you'll end up blading it over the green.

So take out that 6 iron, make sure your hands are well in front of the ball, and just run it up gently.

If you absolutely have to use a wedge to get over a trap, then keep your hands well in front of the ball, as this will make sure you strike the ball with the thin edge of the wedge first, which is what you want.

10. WHAT IS THE BEST QUICK WARM-UP ROUTINE BEFORE A ROUND?

The professionals place great value in warming up properly before a round, so the obvious thing would be to do the same if you want to play better golf.

The pros usually spend at least an hour or an hour and a half warming up before a round.

Granted, the average golfer doesn't always have this much time.

Most weekend golfers play really badly for the first five holes and then start to play better as the round progresses purely because they're now properly warmed up.

Usually they dash off from work, arrive at the golf club, and rush to the first tee without a proper warm-up, or at best having rushed off a few putts on the practice green.

So I'm always going to suggest that you do your best to get in a proper warm-up on the range and then the practice green.

My warm-up routine involves some stretching exercises first to get my body loose. Then I'll start with my clubs, beginning with the shorter clubs and working up to the long irons and driver.

If you really can't get a proper warm-up in and you want something quick, then I'd suggest you take two clubs and swing them right-handed 10 times and left-handed 10 times. That will loosen you up quite quickly.

But again, it's no substitute for a proper warm-up if you're serious about your game.

11. I'VE NEVER BEEN ABLE TO PLAY A FADE OR A DRAW. WHAT ARE THE SECRETS TO THESE SHOTS?

What you are referring to is what golfers call an ability to work the ball.

When you hear of a golfer being described by commentators as "he has every shot in the book," then most often what they're referring to is his ability to work the ball both ways through either a fade or a draw.

A mistake a lot of amateurs make is that when they want to play a fade, they aim their whole body to the left. Unfortunately, this makes them hook the ball because inevitably the clubface is closed.

To hit a fade, the clubface needs to be open.

So it's not good enough to simply open your stance. You also need to open the clubface. This is what allows the clubface to cut the ball and give it that clockwise spin that allows it to fade. You're putting sidespin on the ball.

To hit a fade, you want to have a weaker grip. So you need to shift your hands more to the left, to the point where you may only see one knuckle on your left hand as you grip the club.

Then open your stance by aiming to the left of the target. But don't make the mistake of aiming your clubface left of the target, as well. Your clubface must still face the target, but you will just be opening it more.

When you want to hit a draw, you just do the opposite.

Your grip needs to be stronger, so shift your hands to the right to the point where you can see at least three knuckles on your left hand.

Then you close your stance by aiming more to the right of the target, and the clubface should be closed at impact.

That's the theory behind these shots, but the only way you become proficient at them is to practice.

12. HOW DO I PLAY AN IRON SHOT FROM OUT OF A DIVOT?

My friend and a magnificent golfer, Simon Hobday, used to always arrive at a great drive he had hit, and, when seeing it lying in a divot on the fairway, he'd look up to the sky, shake his hands, and shout, "Play fair!"

I love that.

There is perhaps no greater act of self-pity on this planet than a golfer who finds his ball lying in a divot in the fairway.

When it came to balls in divots, or in other difficult lies, I taught myself to appreciate the benefits of such a challenge.

I always felt that a difficult lie brought out something better in my game because it made me focus better on the shot at hand.

How often have you hit a great drive, have the perfect lie, and then maybe you duff your second?

More often than not, it's the easy shots that we feel we should nail where we sometimes make the biggest mistakes. I believe it's because we're not focused enough, or our concentration is not what it should be as when we are faced with a difficult shot.

So, the first thing I would tell you to do when faced with playing a shot out of a divot is to change your attitude and see it as a blessing to snap your focus back and bring out the best in your game.

Then, make sure the ball is lined up in the middle of your stance. I sometimes even place the ball a little back in my stance so that my clubface is closed. Don't make the mistake of opening your clubface in the belief that this will lift the ball out of the divot.

What you want to do is *play* the ball out of the divot, not try and lift it out.

So don't scoop.

With a slightly closed clubface and your weight favoring your left foot, you'll hit down on the ball.

You need to hit down on the ball, and try and hit the ball first. Your aim is to try and squeeze it out of the divot.

And don't expect miracles. There are times when you can't even hit a good shot from a ball on a peg, so don't expect to hit the greatest shot of your life from a divot.

This kind of realism is something I find so many amateur golfers lack.

I've played in pro-ams for 64 years, and the average golfer never wants to take his or her punishment.

When in divots or bad lies, take your punishment and try and salvage a bogey. It's the doubles and triples that hurt your score.

13. WHEN I SUDDENLY START TO PLAY BADLY DURING A ROUND, IS THERE ANYTHING I CAN DO JUST TO TRY AND KEEP MY GAME TOGETHER, OR GET IT BACK ON TRACK?

Whenever I found that my game was starting to suffer, I used to walk a little slower.

The aim was just to try and calm myself down a bit. By walking slower and breathing a bit more relaxed, I found I could center myself again and regain my rhythm.

I would do this any time I felt my rhythm had been affected by anything that might have thrown me off during my round.

The other thing to remember is that when you're having trouble with your swing during a round, it usually has something to do with the fact that you're decelerating through the golf ball.

When you're hitting it well, you're accelerating through the ball correctly.

The faults start to come in when you decelerate through the ball, and the reason you're doing this can be because you're focused on something else that's happening around you.

So get your mind back on accelerating through the golf ball. The mistake a lot of amateur golfers make is to start theorizing too much when they start to play badly.

When you are playing badly is not the time to start overhauling your swing and making sweeping changes. Leave that for the practice range afterwards. If things start to go south during your round, it's best to get back to the basics as quickly as possible.

These basics include keeping your left arm straight on your backswing and your right arm straight on your follow-through, keeping your head steady, and as I've said, remembering to accelerate through the ball.

To sum up—walk slower, relax, and hit through the ball and not at it.

14. WHAT ARE THE BEST EXERCISES YOU WOULD RECOMMEND FOR A GOLFER TO STAY FIT AND STRONG?

I could write a book on this alone.

Exercise has always been a very big part of my life.

My brother, Ian, instilled this in me very early on in my life, and the fact that I am still competing in tournaments in my 80s is testament to its benefits.

First of all, you need to take into account your age and level of fitness and do the appropriate exercise.

In general, though, my motto is to keep moving. Always keep moving. Rest is rust.

It's important that you have the energy to walk 18 holes and feel good.

I used to play 36 holes at Augusta National and not feel a thing. Now I play 18 holes there, and I can definitely feel it.

Sam Snead was a great walker. I used to marvel at how effortlessly he walked a golf course.

So I'd say start with walking on the treadmill. I'll be honest, I'm not a great fan of jogging because I feel it hurts my joints. So I'd start with getting on the treadmill and becoming walking fit. Swimming is a great exercise, too.

Crunches are another important exercise for golf. Everybody talks about core exercises these days as if it's something new. Well, it's not. I was doing core exercises back when I won the career Grand Slam in 1965, and before this.

I've always focused on my core because I felt it strengthened my back and gave me power in my swing. So sit-ups or stomach crunches are key.

I remember going to a chiropractor, and he said, "You shouldn't be able to walk. You've hit millions of golf balls in your life, and your spine shouldn't be holding up." I know for a fact that it's because of my strong core that I've managed to stay in such good shape.

I'd also include swinging a weighted club into your exercise routine. A weighted club is perfect because it strengthens only golf muscles. You must swing it both ways to ensure a balanced muscle development. This might just be the very best training device ever invented, yet very few people or pros use it.

I think too many young golfers today are focused on exercises that make them look good but have little use in golf. It doesn't help in golf to have big biceps or great pectoral muscles.

Henry Cotton once told me that a golfer's hands, fingers, and wrists could never be too strong. There are a number of ways you can exercise these parts of your body.

Grip a golf club and lift it up and down; rotate it using only your wrist. This will work your wrists and forearms. Squeezing a tennis ball is another effective way to strengthen your hands and forearms, and it's a lot cheaper than a gym membership.

I don't focus too much on bench press exercises. I still prefer a good old-fashioned push-up to strengthen my chest.

And I don't lift heavy weights. I'd rather go with less weight and more repetitions.

I'm a great believer in exercising every part of my body, although I accept that the average golfer doesn't have the time for this.

Speaking of time, there are many ways that you can incorporate your training into daily life.

When it comes to endurance, be opportunistic and choose to take the stairs instead of an elevator or escalator.

As long as you are always thinking about your health, you'll take care of your health.

I also have a number of stretching exercises that I do, as suppleness is another key element in golf success. I do various stretches for my neck, shoulders, forearms and wrists, spine, lats, hamstrings, quadriceps, hip flexors, and groin.

I have found many weird and wonderful ways to exercise when I've been on the road, whether it be in a hotel room or out in a park.

If your desire is there to look after your body, then you will do whatever it takes. And this includes what you put into your body.

This is my general exercise routine. I haven't put any specific numbers to this because I think that is something you need to establish for yourself in terms of where your fitness level currently stands:

- Various leg, lower back, and neck stretching.
- Sets of walking lunges.
- Mixed sit-ups and crunches (the last set done with extra weights).
- Several core exercises.
- Weighted wrist roles.
- Leg presses and squats.
- Various dumbbell exercises. Light weights, lots of reps.
- Sprints on the treadmill with short breaks in between.
- Swing a heavily weighted club 100 times both right-handed as well as left-handed.

My strength workout includes 20–25 repetitions of lunges and squats, forward and reverse, with 20-pound dumbbells.

I also like to exercise outdoors wherever I can. On my farm in South Africa, I built 200 steps into the hillside, and I'll often alternate between jogging, walking, and taking two steps at a time up this hill. I also swim for about 30 minutes while holding onto a paddleboard and using just my legs.

A final key ingredient of my daily workout is 20–30 minutes of meditation. I've always believed in training the mind as much as the body.

15. HOW DO I PLAY A SHOT FROM AN UNEVEN LIE, WHERE MY FEET ARE EITHER ABOVE OR BELOW THE BALL?

What you need to remember is that whichever way the ground slopes, that's the way the ball will go.

So if you are standing with your right foot below your left on a hill, the ball will go high. And if your left leg is lower than your right on a downslope, the ball will go low. It sounds obvious, yet so many golfers forget to make these little adjustments.

If your feet are below the ball, then aim a bit right of the hole to counter the fact that your feet will pull the club more left.

And if your feet are above the ball, aim a bit more left of the hole, as the ground will cause a natural fade to your shot.

Remember to take into consideration which club you hit, as well. For example, if you're playing on a steep upslope, take an extra club to counter the fact that you're going to hit the ball high and as such lose a bit of distance. Similarly, when the ball is below your feet it's going to be a low shot so you may have to take less club than normal.

If the ball is above your feet, grip the club shorter. And if it's below, grip it to its maximum length.

16. WHEN I HIT IT INTO THE ROUGH OR TREES, I ALWAYS FIND MYSELF WANTING TO TAKE ON THE IMPOSSIBLE SHOT. WHAT WOULD BE YOUR STRATEGY HERE? SAFE PLAY OR TAKING ON THE SHOT?

Get out of there and don't lose two and three shots.

Most weekend golfers don't practice enough to take on the impossible shot that the professionals take on and pull off.

I remember reading about Martin Kaymer playing in a pro-am with his father, and how he watched his father and caddie debate about taking on a particularly risky shot that not even he would consider. Kaymer said it was interesting to see his father even consider this shot, when he as a professional and Major winner would not have dreamt of taking it on.

My advice would be to take your medicine, get back on the fairway, and start scoring again from there.

17. WHEN MY REGULAR FOUR-BALL STARTS PLAYING BADLY, I OFTEN FIND MY OWN GAME ALSO SUFFERS. HOW DO I STOP THIS FROM HAPPENING AND KEEP FOCUSED ON MY GAME?

Just play with better players. Don't play with bad golfers, and your standard will rise.

I'm joking, of course.

This happens to all of us.

A lot of times the pros will tell you that they fed off their playing partner's great golf and this allowed them to play just as good. But it works both ways. A playing partner who is hacking around or struggling to control both his game and emotions can have just as great an impact on your own game.

The Open Championship was always a great example of this for me.

I used to arrive at an Open Championship and the weather would be typically bad, and there would be all these pros

complaining and saying how tough it was going to be. Then you'd throw in a course like Carnoustie, and the pros would be saying how it's just going to be impossible to play that course in the tough conditions.

It can be very easy to get sucked into that kind of negative talk and let it affect your own game, and many professionals did.

I always tried to see it to my advantage. I would tell myself that half the field was already out of the tournament and I didn't have to worry about them, because they'd talked themselves out of it.

Golf is the most difficult sport of all when it comes to the mind. The mind is the single most important thing in golf. You've got to make the adjustment in your mind.

You also need to remember that you don't have to watch every shot your playing partner hits. You're not being rude if you don't watch his golf. Remember, you're busy playing golf, not watching golf. Stay focused on what you need to be doing.

This may also mean tuning out what he says. If it gets too bad, you may have to diplomatically say something to your playing partner.

But I usually tried to find a way just to shut it out because the minute you start engaging on the matter, then it becomes an issue in your mind and it has exactly the effect you don't want it to have, namely, focusing your mind on what your playing partner is doing and not on your own game.

18. I FIND IT VERY DIFFICULT TO CORRECT A FELLOW GOLFER IF I'VE SEEN HER BREAK THE RULES. ANY ADVICE?

In my opinion, the leaders in the game have made the rules too complicated.

I haven't met four people in my life that really know the rules of golf perfectly. The professionals are always calling for a ruling because they don't know them all.

My hope is that one day we'll see a rule book with 15 rules in it.

So for a start, accept that nobody knows the rules of golf perfectly well. Even the best rules officials carry the rule book with them to consult it.

I would gently tell your friend that while you yourself may not be great on the rules of golf, you do think she's made a mistake and that you wouldn't want it to cost her on her round or see her disqualified from a competition as a result.

Suggest what you think she should do in this situation, or call for a rules official to clarify the matter.

But be very clear that you are doing this for her best interest here.

Don't be a smart-ass. Be kind and diplomatic.

19. WHAT IS THE BEST ADVICE YOU WOULD GIVE ANYONE WHO IS CONSIDERING BECOMING A PROFESSIONAL?

See a psychiatrist. Don't even think about it.

I'm only joking.

But seriously, you need to think long and hard before making such a decision.

If you can't win amateur tournaments in your area, how are you going to beat pros? Ensure you have a backup plan in place should things not work out.

And if you can't win amateur tournaments outside of your country, how are you going to beat the world's best professionals?

Many people like to point to Seve Ballesteros and say, "Look at him. He had no amateur career."

Well, if you think you are Seve Ballesteros, one of the most naturally gifted golfers the world has ever seen, then good luck to you.

Otherwise, I'd say you better make very sure, because if you don't make it, it's a waste of your career.

You've got to be awfully talented to be a pro. It's always been like that and always will be. And I don't mean just talented at golf. It may be that you are not a naturally gifted golfer or don't have the skills of the next man, but you have something else going for you in terms of a determination to succeed and never give up.

When I turned professional some of the golf pros I knew said I'd starve. I didn't have a particularly good swing. I wasn't as naturally gifted as some of the professionals out there. But I was determined to outwork anybody in the history of the game, and to never give up.

There are so many sacrifices you have to make. There will be long periods away from family and loved ones.

There will be times of self-doubt and criticism. Times of heavy failure.

You see, you can be a good accountant and you'll make a decent living. You'll provide for your family, have a nice home, maybe even afford a holiday home, put your kids through school and college.

But if you're just a good golf pro, you're dead in the water.

Consider this—out of the millions of golfers out there who are trying to be professionals, only 156 play in The Open Championship each year. Even less tee it up in The Masters.

So be realistic. Now is not the time for pipe dreams. This is a decision that will impact the rest of your life. Be realistic about your talent and your potential. Don't listen to the guy at the club who says you could be a world-beater just because you shot 68 on your home course.

You need to know you can shoot 68 and better on any course in the world, in any weather.

You need to have an ability to enjoy suffering. To enjoy adversity.

You've got to have the mind for what is a very hard career choice.

I learned early in my life that talent will only get you so far in golf.

I have seen so many good players come and go. But what separates the great ones from the rest of the pack?

I believe there are a few things.

As I've said, you need a strong mind. A positive attitude. Determination. Dedication.

Then you need a real passion for what you are doing. I'm not talking about just liking or enjoying what you do. That will be great for when you are playing well. But passion is what keeps you pushing forward when you are playing badly or things just aren't going your way.

You need to enjoy suffering, to make it your friend and to feed off it. Trust me, there will be a lot of suffering on your journey. You need to be able to accept this and the adversities that you will face. If you're the kind of person who is prone to self-pity, well then, stop right now and go and find another career.

I would almost say that you need to look at what the great players have overcome, not what they have achieved, and ask yourself if you have it in you to overcome what they have.

Can you overcome the yips like Bernard Langer or Tom Watson did?

Can you overcome a major mental distraction and sadness like finding out your son is autistic, like Ernie Els has?

Can you overcome a major car accident, and being told you will never walk again, never mind play golf, and go on to win a Major like Ben Hogan did? Can Tiger Woods come back and win a Major after all his setbacks?

Success in sports is more often defined by how much you're willing to suffer to achieve your goals.

So in the cold light of day, ask yourselves these questions.

You are going to have to be more honest with yourself than you've ever been, and certainly a lot more honest than those who love you might be.

20. I AM A PROFESSIONAL GOLFER. WHAT ARE SOME OF THE MENTAL TECHNIQUES YOU USED TO MAINTAIN YOUR FOCUS, OR GET IT BACK IF YOU FELT IT WAS DRIFTING?

This is such a great question because this is, in my opinion, the single most important aspect of success in golf.

The mind is where you become a superstar in this game.

I would make mental adjustments continuously during my rounds.

I'd keep myself positive. Meditation and self-hypnosis are critical.

I'd be realistic about my goals. But set them high.

I would never force the issue. But taking calculated risks is vital.

I'd accept adversity and move on through it.

I played with so many golfers who were way better than me and way more skillful, but I won Majors and they didn't.

Jack Nicklaus wasn't the best striker of a golf ball I ever saw, but he won more Majors than anybody.

The swing is not the thing. The mind gets you out of a bind.

21. WHAT IS THE SECRET TO PUTTING?

If there was a secret, you can bet I wouldn't share it with anybody.

Only kidding.

Putting is the most important part of the game. It's where you score, and it's also where the mind comes into play more than in any other aspect of golf.

Guaranteed, if a golfer has his thoughts on other things, it will show up most clearly in his putting.

I've seen some magnificent putters in my time, and I've seen enough different putting styles to believe there is no single way to putt. Or rather, there is only one way to putt and that's the way that gets the ball in the hole.

Jack Nicklaus used to stab at the ball, but what a great finisher of putts he was.

I used to crouch over and jab my putts, and I consider that at my peak few were as good as me holing putts from inside 10 feet.

Tiger Woods took putting to an entirely different level. I don't think we have ever seen, or will likely ever see again, a golfer who was so completely in control of his putting as Woods during his peak around the year 2000.

I'd go as far as to say we'll never see a continued display of putting prowess like that again.

Jordan Spieth certainly came close in 2015, but even he couldn't maintain it for as long as Woods did.

Bobby Locke was one of the finest putters the game has ever seen. He called putting "A game by itself." He also noted that "There is far more in putting than actually striking the ball."

If Ben Hogan believed the secret to golf was in the dirt, Locke believed the secret to putting was in the fingers. He believed in gripping the putter lightly and with a "delicate touch."

I was often a very aggressive player, but I learned to control this when it came to my putting.

You see, I realized that charging a putt at the hole, or hitting the so-called "positive putt," was the quickest way to lose tournaments.

Locke had a great influence on my thinking around this.

His philosophy was that it is always better to leave a putt a little bit short than to run it past the hole. It seems against everything we are told as golfers. People gasp in horror when they see a putt come up short. You hear sayings such as, "Never up, never in" or "The hole won't come to you."

But frankly, I've never seen a putt hit past the hole go in, either. And I can certainly tell you that on greens such as those at Augusta National Golf Club, I'd far rather come up a few inches short of the hole than run 3 feet—or even more—past it.

But Locke put a lot of thought into why he preferred to leave a putt short. You see, if you hit a putt at just the right speed, it can drop in anywhere in the front of the hole, on the side, or even at the back. If you hit a putt hard, there's only one place it can go in, and that's in the center of the hole.

Locke described this as "the front door and two side doors" approach to putting.

He would think of these three "entrances" each time he lined up a putt, and as such he felt he had three chances to hole a putt.

And that brings me to the next very important aspect of putting—confidence.

Once again, if a player is lacking in confidence, it will show up quite clearly in his putting.

Nothing builds golf confidence like holing putts, and nothing breaks down golf confidence like missing putts.

I was such an ardent believer of this throughout my career that I would even carry it through to how I practiced my putting.

I'd step onto the practice putting green and start with a few short putts of about one foot. Then I'd move back to 2 feet, 3 feet, and so on, eventually getting back to the 30-footers. I'd learned that one way to quickly destroy your confidence is to step onto the putting green, try to make a 30-footer as your first putt, and miss. That's the kind of baggage you don't want to take with you onto the first tee.

Developing my confidence in putting extended to even my downtime in hotel rooms.

In 1956, when I was invited to play in the Ampol Tournament in Melbourne, Australia, I honed my putting confidence in my hotel room.

I was leading the tournament by four shots with one round to play. There was a lot of money on the line—£5000 to the winner, which in those days was significant. I had also made the promise to my then-fiancée Vivienne that if I won we could get married.

So I had a lot riding on a good final round.

And then it rained, and the final round was postponed to Monday. I now had that one thing some golfers hate—time on my hands to think about the next day's round.

It can either drive you crazy, or you can use it productively. So I decided to practice my putting in my hotel room. I made it my mission to drill my putting stroke into my head so that by the time the final round teed off, a smooth putting stroke would be second nature to me. I even visualized the putts going in during the final round.

The funny thing is, there was a connecting door in my hotel room. I used this door to hit my putts against. The next minute it swung open, and standing in front of me was Jack Kramer. He was one of the great tennis players in the game, and the Olympics was going on in Melbourne at the same time as this tournament.

The first thing he shouts out is, "What the hell is going on here?" Then he sees me and says, "Gary, what's wrong with you?"

I said to him, "Jack, I'm leading the tournament by four shots and I'm practicing because I'm going to hole a lot of putts on the final day."

He turned around and said, "Oh, well keep going then mate."

I won the tournament.

Maybe it's because I believe so much in the art of putting that I agree entirely with the rule change to ban anchored putting in golf.

I never liked the anchored putting stroke, or the long putter for that matter.

In my opinion, nerves are a part of putting. How you handle the pressure is what makes a champion.

I do believe that you should keep your head dead still and listen to the ball drop into the hole.

So what is the secret to putting?

Well, as you can see there are many elements to it. But in summing up I'd say the secret lies in being able to do whatever you can, within the rules of golf, to get the ball into the hole. And to do it consistently.

Simple, eh?

PART III

THE
QUESTIONS
OF BUSINESS

In November 1985, I turned 50.

At around the same time, I had a very important meeting. It was with my son Marc.

Marc had spent quite a bit of time becoming a very astute businessman, and observing my career, managers, endorsement deals, and how the sports marketing industry worked. His message was simple. "Your time on the Seniors Tour will be short," he said. Exactly the thing somebody wants to hear when he turns 50, I told him.

"You need to start transcending your golf career and build other related businesses," he added. Marc was speaking more about his vision to grow the Gary Player brand. But being a golfer at heart, I was still focused on what I could achieve on the fairways.

When you turn 50, you run the risk of suffering a kind of mental cutoff in terms of personal and business growth. People start to think about "winding down" to retirement.

But Marc had alerted me to the fact that there was another phase to my life—my business life. It's not something I really thought much about. To be honest, I still thought of myself as the same guy who worked his tail off to be a world champion golfer.

Yet after my conversation with Marc, I remember sitting in my study and looking down at a pair of hands that were calloused from all the golf balls hit over the years. By most standards, this pair of hands had conquered quite a bit in the game of golf. But there was still more to achieve.

It was a goal I could relate to because I have always believed in lifelong learning. For me, one of the pillars of longevity—alongside physical and nutritional health—is an ever-curious mind.

Even at the age of 81 I am constantly asking questions. My friends and family know me as somebody who is always inquisitive about life, and so they will often send me interesting articles about anything from politics to sports to spirituality.

I simply don't believe there is a cutoff to learning.

So with Marc's challenge, he awakened in me a new desire for success in business.

I have never been blessed with the great business acumen of others. I remember in 1965 having to decide between a golf club endorsement deal with a company that produced fiberglass shafts and one that made steel shafts.

It came to the point where I had both companies' representatives in front of me. So the steel shaft man says that it's possible to twist the heads off fiberglass shafts, and he grabs one of his competitor's clubs and does so. The other man, shocked to his boots, says steel shafts bend too easily, and he grabs one of the steel-shafted clubs and bends it over his knee. They both continued to mangle each other's clubs right in front of me. It was the most hilarious thing I'd ever seen. My agent at the time, Mark

McCormack, and I just stood there watching these guys destroy each other's clubs.

In the end, I took the more lucrative fiberglass deal and managed to win the 1965 US Open with them. But I knew I couldn't play well with them in the long run, so I ended up not renewing the deal.

At one stage of my career, I also owned a timber farm in the Cape Province of South Africa. Can you imagine? Gary Player the timber merchant.

But what I may lack in business acumen I more than make up for in experience. Here I can bring values such as common sense and patience to any boardroom. Golf has taught me these qualities. It's taught me to know when to be aggressive and when to be conservative. It's taught me how to know when to play the right shot at the right time, and not to be in a hurry to make a decision. It has taught me the value of punctuality. Be late for a tee-off time and you're out of the tournament. Be late for a business meeting and you lose the deal. These are all qualities that have become a habit of my life in business. I didn't learn them in any university or through any great degree. I was taught them on the golf course.

And this is what I brought to the second phase of my career—some wisdom and good experience. I learned some valuable lessons, as well.

Marc has been instrumental in developing the business side of Black Knight International. He has always been very interested in the business side of golf, and the questions surrounding brands and their longevity. I've seen Marc at his happiest when he is standing around under the big oak tree in front of the Augusta National Golf Club, networking with everybody, doing deals and making sure that the Gary Player brand remains as globally relevant as it always has been.

Thanks to Marc, Black Knight International now houses our golf course design company, a real estate development company, a merchandise and apparel business, a tournament business for our global Gary Player Invitational charity series, and The Player Foundation, through which all of our philanthropic and charitable efforts are driven.

Marc was 24 when he started on this journey with me, and it's been amazing to watch him and the business grow. After studying sports marketing, he got his foot in the door working for Mark McCormack at IMG. He then decided to branch out on his own and went to Mark with a very solid proposal of representing me off the golf course while leaving IMG to handle all the on-course business. Looking back on it now, Marc is a visionary, and I would simply not be in the position I am without him.

Back when this conversation had begun, upon my reaching the half-century mark, the traditional model at the time stated that I was finished. I was a fading star, so to speak. But Marc saw the business potential in the Gary Player name and brand. I was also far from ready to retire. I couldn't contemplate society telling me I had reached retirement age when I was still winning golf tournaments. Marc's timing was also brilliant because the senior tour hadn't arrived yet. Tiger Woods hadn't come along yet. So there was a bit of a lull. It's also important to remember that designing golf courses wasn't such a big business then, either. Designers weren't being given $3 or $4 million for a golf course that very quickly became the norm in later years. They were lucky if they were receiving between $250,000 and $500,000.

And then the senior tour hit, and suddenly players such as myself had a second playing career. I won more than 50 senior tour events all around the world as well as a further nine senior

Majors. I became the first golfer in history to win the career Grand Slam on the regular and senior tour. The timing could not have been better. My playing career was extended at exactly the time we were launching my business career.

Marc was the one who really capitalized on the fact that I had travelled so much throughout my career. He showed me that my greatest strength was that I was an international brand. I wasn't seen as an American or British player. I was seen as golf's global ambassador, and that makes it a lot easier to do business in countries such as Japan, China, India, or the UAE.

We've designed almost 400 golf courses in 37 countries and on five continents. The same qualities that defined me as a player are part of my philosophy when it comes to golf course design. I want to be the best.

I've made good business decisions thanks to the great team I have around me. And then there was the time I decided to try and go into the music business.

Recording an album of country songs was perhaps not the smartest business decision I ever made. It was called *Sing Along with Gary Player*. But hey, it was a lot of fun. And it sold out, as well.

Ben Hogan had his Five Fundamentals for the golf swing. So I decided that in business I would draw up my own set of fundamentals—my Ten Commandments. They are:

1. Change is the price of survival.
2. Everything in business is negotiable except quality.
3. A promise made is a debt incurred.
4. For all we take in life we must pay.
5. Persistence and common sense are more important than intelligence.

6. The fox fears not the man who boasts by night, but the man who rises early in the morning.

7. Accept the advice of those who love you, though you like it not at present.

8. Trust instinct to the end, though you cannot render any reason.

9. The heights by great men reached and kept were not attained by sudden flight, but they, while their companions slept, were toiling upward in the night.

10. There is no substitute for personal contact.

The key to longevity in golf is a solid foundation, and it's the same in business. I realized that as long as your foundation is strong, you can build into any new area of your life that you wish. The strength of your foundation determines the heights of your success.

So while I might not ever have had a strong business background in terms of studying business or getting some academic qualification in business, I have learned that you cannot put a price on experience—or instinct—when it comes to business.

I'm a great believer in that gut feeling that we call instinct.

This was a lesson my father taught me through a very simple story.

One day I asked my father, "Who's the best friend you ever had?" He said, "A rat." I was flabbergasted. Then he said that when he worked in the mines, he'd be sitting there underground with these massive rats.

The miners always gave these rats a piece of their sandwiches, because anytime there was any caving in, the rats came running out. And that's instinct. In business, I love the advice to always trust your instinct even though you're not sure why at the time. So one day my father and his fellow miners saw all these rats come running out, and they also ran for their lives. The mineshaft caved in. But they were safe.

1. I RUN A BUSINESS WHERE A NUMBER OF OPPORTUNITIES COME MY WAY ON A DAILY BASIS. BUT I'M NEVER REALLY SURE WHICH OPPORTUNITIES ARE RIGHT FOR ME TO PURSUE AND WHICH I SHOULD PASS ON. HOW DO YOU DECIDE WHICH OPPORTUNITIES TO SAY YES TO?

There may well be a number of opportunities coming your way in a week, but that doesn't mean they are all opportunities for you.

You've got to look at what your foundation is. What have you built your business on?

Just as there are certain fundamentals to the basic golf swing, there are fundamentals to your business that have generated the success you enjoy.

Identify clearly what these fundamentals are, and then you'll be able to see whether the opportunities that come your way fit into this or not.

For example, when I was at the end of my playing career and was starting to focus more on business, I had certain fundamentals on which I wasn't willing to compromise.

What built my success on the golf course was going to be the foundation for my success in business.

You also need to be honest with yourself when assessing various opportunities.

There was a time that we experimented with the wine business. We produced some very good wine, and let's face it, most professional golfers have their own wine label these days. So it seemed an obvious opportunity to expand into.

The whole concept behind the wine was to create a Major Championship Series of wine reflecting my nine Majors on the regular tour.

Each limited series of wine was dedicated to one of my Major victories, and each had a specially designed label, beginning with the first vintage—the 1959 Muirfield collection commemorating my Open Championship victory there.

We had a lot of fun with the wine, which we produced in partnership with Quoin Rock Vineyards in the top wine-growing region of Stellenbosch in South Africa.

I remember the launch of our second vintage in 2011, Augusta 1961, which we timed to coincide with the 50th anniversary of my Masters victory in 1961.

We travelled to the Vineyard Wine Market in Augusta, Georgia, where I met wine enthusiasts and golf fans and signed the bottles for them. I think I must have signed over 600 battles during Masters week.

We also distributed the wine in Hong Kong and China.

I am very health-conscious and not much of a drinker. I may have a whisky now and then, or even a rare beer. But I am pretty much a teetotaler. My son Marc was well aware of this when he pursued the idea for the wine.

As Marc said about the venture, he wasn't about to now go out and try and convince the world that his teetotaling father was a wine connoisseur. He admits his own reluctance to the idea at the time. But then he decided it would be a limited exclusive series that would honor the Majors of my career and not try to be anything beyond this. And he also said something that made me buy into it. "Let's just have fun with it," he told me. "But still only produce the very best quality."

So we did.

And I must say, I was quite proud of the fact that our first vintage in 2003 and the resultant wine received a four-star rating by the John Platter Wine Guide, one of the world's most respected wine guides.

I particularly liked their description of the wine—"Well made, befitting Gary Player's ethos." That's what I want to hear, whether we are in the business of golf course design, wine, our own brand of health tea, clothing, or whatever we choose to pursue under the Gary Player or Black Knight brands.

When I went into the horse business, many people thought I was mad. I was told that oft-quoted line, that a wise man never buys something that eats while he sleeps. But they never truly understood the background here.

Shortly after turning professional at the age of 17, I bought a horse called Judy. I used to ride her around the golf course near our home in Johannesburg and spend hours grooming and feeding her.

It was my desire to breed thoroughbred racehorses that led me to buying my farm in Colesberg. The water there has this ideal blend of calcium and phosphorous, which is perfect for developing strong bones in racehorses. So when that opportunity arose, it was a perfect fit in the overall business picture I had.

My love for horses began while I was at school. I had a friend, Frank Hodgkinson, who lived on a beautiful farm in Fourways, also near Johannesburg. He would invite me to spend weekends with him, and we used to ride their horses together. I'd been around horses before, mostly at the local Turffontein racetrack, where I used to sell programs to earn a bit of extra money. But riding the horses on Frank's farm is where I really developed my deep love for horses. I'll never forget that feeling, climbing onto a horse for the first time and the raw power of the animal as it galloped off. It felt just like the cowboys I admired so much. I was hooked, and it's a passion that has run alongside my golf throughout my life. So much so that now I'd much rather talk about horses than golf. When I travel I study genealogies of horses. I can't get enough of it.

Those weekends on Frank's farm are also what led me to the pursuit of my dream of buying my own farm one day. I lead a very busy life and yes, I do love people and travelling. But I often have this need to be in quiet places close to nature.

When my mom died, I spent a lot more time with Frank at their farm. We'd ride all day, then we'd wipe the sweat off the horses and wash them. So my business plan for this aspect of my career was starting to take shape very early in my life.

But when you talk about following the right opportunities, I did make a few mistakes along the way to prove that even though it looks like a right fit, it doesn't mean it is always right for you.

When I went to America I visited a few farms there, and on one of them they put me on the back of a quarter horse. I just had to sit on its back, and the horse did all the work cutting the cattle. I was so impressed by this horse, and I fell in love with it. So in 1964, I shipped 60 of them back to South Africa. They arrived at Cape Town Harbour, and there was quite a bit of interest. People were wondering what Gary Player was doing bringing 60 American Quarter Horses into South Africa. So there were a few people on the dock that day when the horses arrived. One of them, a young girl, walked up to me on the dock and asked me about the horses. So I said to her, "Do you like horses?" I didn't know it at the time, but the girl was Gonda Butters (later Gonda Betrix). She was already a promising rider and show jumper. By that stage she already had her national colors for South Africa in show jumping, and she would go on to become an icon of horse

riding in South Africa. And here I was asking if she was interested in horses.

At that stage we had another farm in Magoebaskloof, which lies in the Limpopo province of South Africa. Unfortunately, the quarter horses never really took off in South Africa, and I learned later that Magoebaskloof is not a good area for horses because of the high rainfall there. The farm, though, was an absolute paradise. It was located on a timber plantation on a hill, and the morning mist used to roll in through the valleys. But when we started moving over to thoroughbreds, we soon realized that the area was detrimental to their health. We had horses being born with crooked legs because they weren't receiving the right nutrients. We used to get over 80 inches of rainfall a year there, and the grass was green. But it was useless because it didn't have the nutrients that a thoroughbred needs. There was also no limestone in the ground, which is another important element for thoroughbreds. I wanted to pursue the thoroughbred horses, so I decided to sell the farm. And that's when we moved to the farm in the Karoo.

The bones of the horses we have bred there are so much stronger. Their feet, where you cut the hooves, are so much tougher. And because of the quality of the water there, the hearts of these horses are so much stronger. The Karoo has bred some champion horses.

My first thoroughbred was a horse called Prussian Pride, and I started this side of my business with him and a few other mares. Soon I had over 200 horses. Mark McCormack thought I was mad but indulged my passion because he knew it would help me to recharge my batteries off the golf course.

Even Seve Ballesteros said to me, "My friend, why are you so interested in horses? There's no money in horses." I said to him, "Seve, if you win The Masters and I win the Kentucky Derby, there is no comparison in how much more money I will collect over the years."

We had a horse, Mowgli, that won the Durban July, one of our greatest races in South Africa. We had another horse, Lady Windermere, which as a mare won two Group Ones (the highest level of thoroughbred racing in most countries).

We once had a horse by the name of IpiThombi. Her father was my stallion. What a horse. It was really a rags-to-riches story with her, much like my own career. She came out of Zimbabwe and had no future there as the country began its sad downward slide under the leadership of Robert Mugabe. She was sold for about $85 and went on to make millions. She became one of the greats of thoroughbred racing, winning big races in South Africa, Dubai, and America.

I felt a strong bond with that horse because, like me, it won in different places around the world. But I just love those kinds of stories, where the underdog really comes through. The horse world is full of such tales. There was also Jet Master, another great South African thoroughbred. This horse was sold for about $1,300 and went on to become a champion. Then it went to stud, and they were charging $22,000 for every time it covered a mare.

We've been blessed with many champions from the Karoo. It used to be *the* place in South Africa for thoroughbred breeding. But then some of the pioneer farmers there died, and slowly that era faded away. Now it's down to about six or seven breeders. And it's shifted to the Western Cape, which is where South Africa's best breeders are now based. But I am very proud to still be one of the few good breeders in the Karoo.

My passion for horses consumes my life now. No matter where I am in the world, I phone the stud farm sometimes three or four times a day checking up on the horses. I even want to know if they're watering my trees there. I think I was very fortunate to discover a love for something outside of golf. So many great sportsmen come to the end of their careers and then get bored because they have nothing else with which to occupy their time. I can't find enough time in the day for what I still want to do. I'm up at five o'clock in the morning starting to work with the horses, and I can be busy on the farm all day.

My horses and my farm in Colesberg bring me an immense peace. I have always taken pleasure in the simple things in life.

Opportunities will come your way every single day. When it comes to selecting which opportunities are right for you, it's not enough simply to ask whether they will make money and then pursue those. Money is not enough of a driving force in the long term. You really do need to feel something for the opportunities you are looking at.

I have always been drawn to horses because of their athleticism. I mean, you see a foal born, and within a few minutes it is up on its feet and running around the paddock. It's an incredible animal. Maybe I see something of myself in that drive and determination of a horse.

And just like my horse business, your opportunities need to augment your overall business picture. I started with a horse and ended up with a farm, as well, that has given me so many other pleasures, because the farm enhanced what I was doing with my horses.

Another thing I love about horses is that you can breed a champion sire with a champion mare, and it doesn't mean you are going to produce another champion horse. And then you can have a champion horse coming from absolutely nothing. There is no hard and fast rule. You like to think you know what you're doing, and you have your own taste for various horses. I also study the genetics of these horses, and I probably spend an hour a day reading up and studying these. I spend so much time with it that even my wife Vivienne can tell you about thoroughbred bloodlines. Sometimes I even think she should be the farm manager, she knows so much about it herself.

But that unpredictability about what makes a champion horse is also the beauty of golf for me.

For example, if you go to the 10 best players in the world for a golf lesson, most of them will tell you something different. It's the same with horses. You can try and pair a myriad of champions together, and you'll always get something different.

It sounds a lot like golf. And it certainly sounds a lot like the story of my career.

It's also a good example to bear in mind when deciding on which opportunities to pursue. What may at first seem like the perfect fit often turns out to be the opposite. And sometimes, the opportunity that comes your way when you weren't really looking for it could turn out to be the best one of all.

2. HOW DID YOU ENABLE YOUR BUSINESS TO BECOME SOMETHING THAT COULD STAND ON ITS OWN AND OUTLAST YOU?

My son Marc and our team at Black Knight have been instrumental in creating this and focusing on building our brand for the last 30 years.

It is always a concern, when you have created something around one person, how that business will continue when that person is no longer there.

What Marc spotted very early on is the potential to build a brand that will outlast the individual. You need to identify what your brand is and then build on that.

Marc has often said of today's top young golfers that they need to figure out who they are, not in the esoteric sense of the word, but in the brand sense.

As he points out, we know who Gary Player is. We know who Jack Nicklaus is. But who is Rory McIlroy or Jordan Spieth? What do they stand for and what do they represent?

And Marc was always very clever about managing this. He didn't license the Gary Player name out to everyone with a check-book or big wallet. It may have meant a lot more short-term money with that kind of mass-market approach, but it wasn't within his picture of building our brand. He did not want me to become the

Pierre Cardin of golf like Arnold Palmer, because that didn't fit with who I was.

He built the business around everything that is Gary Player. What I believe in. How I dress. The use of the color black. The traveler, the rancher, the fitness fanatic. Quality over quantity.

For example, look at The Masters.

Every year during The Masters we rent a house, which for that week becomes Gary Player central.

Then Marc invites potential clients or current business partners from around the world to join us for that week. It's a tremendous marketing opportunity for us. And why does it work so well? Because it fits the Gary Player brand. I am widely known as a person who loves people and loves to engage with people. So let's rent a house and engage with people during one of the biggest weeks in golf, and give them an unforgettable experience. They spend time with me. We play golf together. We have dinner together. We watch the final round together, with me providing my own brand of commentary.

We do business the Gary Player way—spending time with people and through personal contact. It's personal, which is how I have always run my career and business. When I make a commitment to a sponsor, I give them my all. I want a personal connection with them. That's who I am, and that's become my brand. If you had tried the same with Ben Hogan, for example, it wouldn't have worked. The Ben Hogan brand represented something else in people's minds.

For your brand to outlast you, you need to work at it every day. Marc admits that he spends every day thinking, "What do we do when Gary Player is gone?"

He often jokes that he doesn't like to tell me, but there will come a day when I will die. Then what?

As Marc points out, then you have to make sure the foundation of your brand is in place.

He often uses the example of Bobby Jones and Augusta National. Jones is long gone physically, but Augusta National is still thriving, and so too is its apparel and everything around it. And people are still buying books about Bobby Jones and are interested in that story.

So identify what your brand is, and what you represent or stand for. Then build that. Think of Ralph Lauren, Coco Chanel, and René Lacoste. What do they stand for?

My brand is all about hard work, perseverance, determination, longevity, healthy living, and a belief that retirement is simply not an option. As I've said before, rest is rust. My brand is also about caring for underprivileged children, and this will go on long after I'm dead through The Player Foundation.

That is not just a business than can last. It's a legacy, and it's a far more important goal to strive for.

3. FOR YEARS, MY BUSINESS WAS A LEADER IN ITS FIELD. NOW OTHER BUSINESSES HAVE STARTED TO EMULATE WHAT WE DO, AND SOME ARE DOING IT CHEAPER AND I'VE LOST A FEW CLIENTS TO THEM. WOULD YOU DROP YOUR PRICE TO KEEP THE BUSINESS?

Change is the price of survival.

The world is in a state of economic flux. We're seeing it all around us. Brexit has thrown up an entirely new business landscape in Europe. Asia has slowed down economically, and it's affecting the rest of the world.

Companies are being forced to reassess the way they do business, because what worked yesterday is not working today and certainly won't work tomorrow.

And there is nothing wrong with this. You may just find that the changing business landscape is opening up new avenues for you, or perhaps showing you that your business does indeed need to change from what it has always been.

Take a look at Nike.

In 2016, after 15 years of trying to sell golf equipment, Nike Golf shut down. And it made perfect sense. Nike has never been known for golf equipment. It is essentially a footwear and apparel company. So they shut down what had for years been a side of their business that really struggled to make a significant impact in the golf equipment market.

At the same time, they bolstered their true business strength by signing world No. 1 Jason Day to a multiyear $10 million annual deal to wear Nike apparel.

To have a business that stands the test of time, you need to keep moving with the times.

The golf industry is very quick to say it is in a slump that has been helped by the lack of a force in the game such as Tiger Woods. Analysts argue that the Tiger Woods effect was of inestimable worth to the industry as a whole.

Of course, there is an element of truth to this. But it doesn't tell the whole story.

Tiger helped golf in ways that Jack Nicklaus or Arnold Palmer also helped golf. But Tiger's best years also happily coincided with a period of tremendous financial prosperity around the world.

Business is a lot like the golf swing in that timing is critical.

So to come back to your question, I would start by looking at why you were a success in the first place. What did you do that made your business so successful and sought after, to the point that others started to copy you?

Chances are that you saw a gap in the market and filled it by adding value. So why can't you do that again?

It's not as simple as just dropping your price to match the now-cheaper competition. Undercutting on price is an age-old business practice, and in the long run nobody wins in a price war. It's bad for business all around.

But you can win by adding value.

You can keep your price the same, but tack on far more value. So that's what you need to be thinking—how can I add the kind of value my competitors cannot match?

Anybody can compete on price, but not just anybody can compete on value.

In tough economic times, consumers are looking for added value. They're not necessarily looking for cheaper. But they definitely do want to get more value for their money.

Give them this value, and you should be able to win back those clients who see something in your business that your competition cannot match.

Look at our Gary Player Invitational series of charity tournaments around the world. As I've said, these are tough economic times, and companies are cost-cutting everywhere. Sponsorships are always one of those areas where companies cut first.

Yet we have been able to double the sponsorship of one of our major Gary Player Invitational partners, Berenberg Bank. Why? Because we add value and can clearly demonstrate it to the sponsor.

I give them more of my personal time. We invite them to The Masters. We find more and more ways that we can offer greater value for them.

Professionally, I have longstanding sponsors that have been with me through economic boom times and slumps.

I'm talking about Rolex, The Coca-Cola Company, SAP, Sun International, Callaway, and now Berenberg Bank. What keeps them on board is the value added. Where other young professionals might sign up for a corporate day and say, "Ok, but I'll only give you three hours," I say, "I'll give you the whole day. I'll shake hands with your clients. I'll teach them how to play golf. I'll tell them stories." That's value.

When we launched our annual Gary Player Invitational tournament in South Africa, we have had occasions where we've done this with a golf day for the media. I don't just stand there, give them a speech, and then let them tee off. No. I go out there and make sure I play at least one hole with every media four-ball during the day. That's value.

That's where professional golf is now heading, namely, with brands searching for meaningful customer engagement for their best clients. The days of just slapping your logo on a good player or athlete and hoping for the best is long gone.

We've expanded our social media efforts because we know the brands that represent an 81-year-old Gary Player are also brands looking to appeal to a teenager.

What the changing face of world economics is showing is that people, especially the younger generation, are searching for real value and an engaging experience. They want that connection that makes them feel like they are getting something special for their hard-earned money. They want to feel as though their money and where they are spending it is appreciated. This will be the competitive advantage for the companies of the future.

Cheaper is only cheaper until the next guy comes along and undercuts you.

Value, service, and quality are the long game in business.

4. WHAT ARE THREE OF THE MOST IMPORTANT BUSINESS LESSONS YOU'VE LEARNED?

It would be difficult to limit it to just three. I have learned an incredible amount from some brilliant financial minds.

One lesson I've learned is to trust my instincts.

Those early deals between agent Mark McCormack and myself, as with some of his other deals, were done purely on a handshake and a shared understanding.

I'm not saying all business should be done this way, and maybe it was a different time. But I've learned to trust that gut feeling.

I often like to use the example of the impala in the African bush. You know, when that impala gets a whiff of trouble, he bolts. He doesn't stick around and start to try and reason it out. "Maybe that's not a lion's scent I'm smelling. Maybe I'm just over-reacting." Nope. When instinct talks, that impala listens. And he lives another day as a result.

I also believe there is no substitute in business for personal contact. My brand is built on the fact that I offer personal contact. People can connect with me.

Another lesson I have learned is that everything in business is negotiable except quality. It is this integrity and mutual respect that I have always tried to apply to my business deals.

Golf is a game bound by certain rules. But of far more importance are its unwritten rules. There are also certainly legalities when it comes to business—what you can and can't do. Then there are the unwritten laws of business.

In golf, the opportunity to cheat is always there, but as golfers we choose not to. And similarly in business, there is always the opportunity to bend the rules, to step into the gray areas. Never compromise on the strict set of values you have for your business.

It's these values that are going to become even more important in the future. As the world stares at the prospect of further economic challenges, it is the businessmen and businesswomen with the fortitude and the character who will be the ones to steer us back onto the straight and narrow.

It is the future directors and CEOs who share these values who will bring stability back to the companies of the world, and as such bring much-needed impetus back to the job market.

The strange thing is, I have never thought of myself as a businessman.

Even on the golf circuit, I have known some pretty clever individuals when it comes to money.

Lee Trevino always used to say that real pressure on the golf course is playing a match for $100 when you only have $10 in your pocket.

Arnold Palmer was a pretty shrewd character. I remember inviting him out to South Africa once, and I took him on a tour of the gold mines. We joined a tourist group and went down this one mine. At the bottom, our host showed us a gold bar on a table and said if anybody could pick it up with just one hand, he could keep it.

Arnold said he'd give it a go. Now Arnold had the strongest hands I've ever seen. He walked up to the table, wrapped his big paw around that gold bar, and lifted it straight up. The host nearly had a heart attack. He couldn't believe it. And when Arnold wanted to take it home with him, he kept pleading for him not to. Now in my book, the Arnold Palmer Gold Business is the one I'd like to be invested in.

Ultimately, my belief is that success in business is so much like the golf swing. In golf, the swing means nothing without a good follow-through. The start of your swing is all about intent. It signifies everything you hope to achieve with this particular shot. But the follow-through is the result.

In business, as in golf, you are judged by what you have done, not what you are about to do or talk about doing.

5. I RUN A SERVICE BUSINESS, AND I FIND IT VERY DIFFICULT TO ASK PEOPLE TO PAY ME WHAT I FEEL I'M WORTH. HOW DID YOU DEAL WITH CLIENTS ALWAYS WANTING YOUR BASEMENT PRICE?

I always remembered my worth.

And I was always honest with myself about what I felt I was worth.

Then, in my mind, there was no questioning or doubting when I charged what I felt I was worth.

It's when you doubt your worth that you allow people to negotiate you down.

In business, people are always going to want to get you down to your basement price or get the most out of you for the least amount of money.

So don't take it as a personal slight.

They have a right to try, and you have a right to say, "No."

If you're finding it difficult to ask clients to pay you what you feel you're worth, then I'd suggest that you are having trouble understanding your worth.

Clearly identify your worth to yourself first, and then you will have no problem conveying this to your clients.

But in doing so, be realistic and be honest with yourself. Don't inflate your worth. And don't define your worth by feelings of resentment or out of a sense of being owed.

That's entitlement, and it's one of the evils of modern society.

We are entitled to nothing.

You are also not entitled to business. You have to earn it. There is no such thing as having paid your dues or any of that nonsense.

Again, that's defining your worth along the wrong lines.

Define what you think you are really worth.

Be confident and believe in your worth.

Then charge your worth and overdeliver.

6. MY BUSINESS IS ALL-CONSUMING, AND I FIND IT'S LEFT ME COMPLETELY BURNT OUT. HOW DO YOU MAINTAIN YOUR DRIVE AND PASSION FOR YOUR WORK?

Balance is as important in life as it is in the golf swing.

It doesn't help that you kill the goose that lays the golden egg. Your business can only succeed for as long as you have the energy to make it succeed.

So you have to look after yourself.

I travel a lot, and believe me, as fit as I am, at the age of 81 it takes a toll. But my business is dependent on me meeting people and traveling the world, so I look after myself. I exercise, I eat healthy, and I make sure I get enough sleep. This means I can be at my best for my business.

I have always been blessed with a great energy in my life. If you have lost your passion and energy, you need to establish why, because that is the key to your longevity.

You may also need to remind yourself what drives you.

I am driven to reach people. I love meeting people all over the world. I love taking the message of healthy living to people everywhere, and I am driven to spread this message across the globe.

Remind yourself what drives you, and you'll start to get that passion back.

I've also always been a great believer in the power of the mind, and as I've said before, often I feel that a simple adjustment of your mind can help make a big difference, as well.

I know how privileged I am to be doing what I do, and I remind myself daily of this privilege.

Gratitude is a big part of my life. It's something I think all golfers can relate to, no matter their skill level. We play an ancient game, and as such we are careful to protect the traditions and etiquette of our sport. When it comes to golf etiquette, there is not another sport where those who practice it are so vigilant in terms of guarding these basic principles of behavior on the course.

And we also know the privilege of being able to play the world's most magnificent golf courses. Even your average weekend golfer will speak in glowing terms of what it was like to play one of the famous golf courses, and despite the fact that he may have played a poor round of golf. Golfers understand gratitude.

That's why I get so angry when I hear today's young professionals complain about being burnt out after three weeks on the road at tournaments. Tell that to the average man who works an entire year for maybe two weeks off on holiday with his family, and see how much sympathy he has for you.

So sometimes, to overcome that feeling of being burnt out, you just need to reset your mind and remind yourself how blessed you are in various areas of your life.

It always works for me.

In the modern world of high-pressure business and international travel, it's also important to know how to travel effectively to ensure you get the best out of yourself after those long trips.

This year marks my 64th consecutive year of air travel. Over that time, I have journeyed more than 16 million air miles around the globe for golf and charity.

In 2016 alone, I logged nearly 400,000 miles of air travel, and we still have three months to go.

I've been to Abu Dhabi, Tokyo, London, New York, Mission Hills in China, and Sun City in South Africa for my Gary Player Invitational series of charity tournaments for underprivileged children.

I have also been to Vietnam, Cuba, Honduras, and Johannesburg for business. I've journeyed to Los Angeles for media engagements, then to Augusta for The Masters Tournament followed by trips to White Sulphur Springs, West Virginia, and Branson, Missouri, for both golf course design projects as well as playing commitments on the Champions Tour.

I returned home to Colesberg in the Karoo of South Africa, where Vivienne and I joined the mayor and some of the residents in a cleanup campaign of the town.

Then there was a quick trip to Cape Town to film a ROLEX documentary of my life, and then off to Frankfurt, Germany, for a sponsor engagement, then to Troon, Scotland, for The Open Championship and a stop in London for an appearance at Wimbledon.

After an official visit to the World Golf Hall of Fame in Palm Beach, Florida, I travelled to Rio de Janeiro as part of the South African Olympic team. New York and then Greenville, South Carolina, followed this.

Air travel is incredibly taxing on the body, and over the years I've refined my travel down to an art to ensure I get the best out of myself and for my sponsors or clients when I land.

I always pack light. A few of the things you'll always find in my bag are a skipping rope, a copy of *Blood Horse Thoroughbred Magazine*, and the latest thoroughbred breeding list of my stud farm. I love to study horse bloodlines.

To counter the effects of jetlag, I stay away from caffeine and alcohol on my flights, and I drink plenty of water to stay hydrated.

My meals on flights will be light and will include fruit, salads, and vegetables. I'll get up regularly during the flight to stretch.

It's amazing how much air travel has changed since I started flying all those years ago.

It used to take us several days to get anywhere. For example, for the 1965 Australian Open, I had to fly from Paris to Melbourne via New York, Los Angeles, Hawaii, Fiji, and Sydney.

I made the flight and arrived three hours before my first-round tee-off time. I went straight to the golf course and ended up winning the tournament by six shots.

7. WHAT, IN YOUR OPINION, ARE THE QUALITIES OF AN EFFECTIVE MANAGER?

He or she must be a good communicator and lead by example.

Honest and open communication is the most effective tool in management.

Look at the great leaders through the ages. The one thing they all had in common was their ability to communicate well with the people they led.

They were able to get the collective buy-in of their followers to believe in a single cause. For example, I recently read a biography of George Washington, who was an incredible leader. He made some monumental mistakes along the way, but he was a fearless leader who could communicate very well.

A singular moment represents this quite well in my mind. When Washington had won the Revolutionary War, Congress was broke and couldn't afford to pay the soldiers what they'd been promised. There was dissent in the ranks and talk of a military coup. Washington decided to meet with these plotters and deliver what many believe is the speech of his life.

But even after he delivered what was a great speech, the men were still angry.

As related in this biography, Washington then removed from his pocket another letter, which he intended to read to the men. And it wasn't the contents of his speech or this other letter that eventually pacified them and won them over.

It was how he did it.

Washington was revered by his men for his selfless style of leadership. He was seen as a true man amongst men. But now, at the age of 51 and clearly weary from many battles—both on the battlefield and in early American politics—he took out this letter and paused. Then he took out his reading glasses, and as the biography notes, he actually apologized to the men watching him in stunned silence, telling them, "I have grown gray in your service and now find myself growing blind."

This simple act of pure honesty completely disarmed the angry gathering. With such an act of honest communication, Washington quite literally rescued the future of the United States of America from becoming a messy political landgrab by an angry militia.

You can only rule by fear for so long before people either stop fearing you or lose respect for you. A manager who rules by fear will never get the best of the people under him or her.

I can't help but think of South Africa's own Nelson Mandela.

How did he rescue a country on the brink of civil war and drive it toward a peaceful resolution? With the right words, at the right time, spoken honestly.

That's what earns people's respect. That's what moves them into positive action.

Look at the great leaders of the past, and in their qualities you will see exactly what it takes to be an effective manager of people in the business world.

A great manager also has to be unafraid to lead.

Let me take you back to a Sunday evening in 2003, when darkness settled over a golf course in South Africa, and two men took an agreement they had both put their signatures to and tore it up. Then they shook hands.

Those two men were Jack Nicklaus and myself. The occasion was the 2003 Presidents Cup in my home country of South Africa. This was the first time I was leading the International Team as captain. Jack was captain of Team USA.

Jack and I have always been fierce competitors, and this was no different. Believe me, we wanted to beat the hell out of each other.

We both had incredibly strong teams. Jack had Tiger Woods and Phil Mickelson leading his team, while I had Ernie Els and Retief Goosen leading mine.

We were playing on a course I knew intimately, The Links at Fancourt, having designed it myself.

But there was a far bigger issue at stake. This was the first Presidents Cup in Africa. I was incredibly proud to be leading a team in my home country, and in front of our then-president, Thabo Mbeki, who attended the matches along with then-president George Bush and Nelson Mandela. It was an important occasion for our young democracy, and another vital step in South Africa's process of regaining its place on the world stage.

So right from the start, this was a Presidents Cup that was always going to be far greater than just the result of a golf tournament. I suppose that's what Jack and I both had in our minds, and which led us to make the decision we eventually did.

But first the golf.

The opening day didn't go as well as I would've liked. We only took 3 ½ of the six available points, but were still up nonetheless. Then on Friday the Americans hit back, winning seven of the 10 points on offer. It was a huge blow. But Ernie Els had won both of the matches he was involved in, and I felt that as he was our leading player, this would at least give us some spirit in the team room.

It certainly did, because on Saturday my players responded like champions. We won all six of our matches in a complete rout of the Americans. It gave us a 12½–9½ lead going into the final day, and all we needed was five points from the remaining 12 singles matches to win the Cup.

The Americans came out fighting and won five of the first six singles to lead the overall match. Retief Goosen then beat Phil

Mickelson 2&1 to see us draw level. We went on to win two of the next three matches, and victory was in sight.

There was always a sense that this was going to be a Presidents Cup decided between Tiger Woods and Ernie Els. In the Singles, Tiger took first blood when he beat Ernie, 4&3.

Then Davis Love III and Robert Allenby halved. That left both teams tied at 17 points each.

The rules stated that each team selects a player for a sudden-death playoff. I selected Ernie. Jack chose Tiger.

Going back to the 18th hole, both players made par. Then they played the first and parred again. On to the second hole. Pars again. It began to grow dark, and it was time for decisions to be made.

I remember Ernie asking me that they keep playing. He was under the impression that in the case of a tie, America would retain the Cup. And he didn't like that at all. He was also desperate to beat Woods, who had gotten the better of him on so many occasions.

But as I said, there were always bigger issues at stake here.

And that's when Jack came over to me for a chat. In the bizarre chaos that surrounded us, we agreed that there shouldn't be a loser to this one. So we agreed to call it a tie, ignoring the contract we had signed that said we should play until a winner is determined. And Jack graciously agreed with me that the Cup would be shared by both teams for the next two years.

PGA Tour commissioner Tim Finchem was there with us, and he agreed with our decision.

I remember Jack telling the media afterwards, "I think some people will be upset with that decision. I think some people will probably pan Gary and me for that decision. But both Gary and I feel in our hearts that was the right thing to do, and we stand by it."

This was one of those great moments in golf when nobody won, and it was perfect.

Find the manager who is unafraid to make those kinds of decisions.

8. HOW DO YOU FIND THE BALANCE BETWEEN PAYING THE BILLS AND DOING WHAT YOU LOVE?

If you can do what you love and pay the bills, well done to you.

If you have to be like the majority of the history of civilization and have a job just as a job, then that's also fine.

I sometimes worry that this quest to find meaning and purpose in work has become a little overdone.

I'm not saying there is anything wrong with wanting to enjoy your work. But sometimes a job is just a job, a means to an end, or a way to pay the bills, as you say. And maybe it doesn't need to be any more than that. Perhaps you find your meaning and passion in other areas of your life.

Not everybody is destined to live out their true purpose in life through their work.

Barack Obama worked in an ice cream shop at one point. What on earth would've happened if he believed he needed to find his purpose only in his work in an ice cream shop?

So I don't think there is a balance between paying the bills and doing what you love. I don't think they're mutually exclusive. I think you could pay the bills and do what you feel you need to do here, and then do what you love in other areas of your life.

And again, if you do somehow find a way to make these two paths merge, then well done. If not, then it's also perfectly fine to earn a living one way and earn a life another.

I have a worker on my farm who has never missed a day of work in his life with me. He drives a tractor, and we sometimes work together planting trees or mending fences. I don't think he ever sits and dwells about the purpose of his life in his work. But you know what? The example he sets by being such a great worker is something I tell people about around the world. When I address companies, I tell them about this man's incredible work ethic.

Never forget, sometimes paying the bills can be the greatest act of service you can do and, like the worker on my farm, can set an example that can inspire hundreds of people.

9. I'M JUST STARTING A BUSINESS, AND SOME CLIENTS ARE TELLING ME THEY CANNOT PAY ME BUT WILL "OPEN DOORS" FOR ME WHERE THEY CAN. HOW DO I HANDLE THIS?

If that open door leads to somebody who is going to pay you, great. If not, then you don't really have a business.

I've been in the sponsorship and endorsement game my whole life, and people will often promise you the world if you just do this or do that for them. But promises don't buy nappies, which in my case there were a lot to buy in the beginning of my career.

People who really see value in what you do will be willing to pay for it. I would be wary of anything else.

10. WHAT IS YOUR STRATEGY DURING A NEGOTIATION PROCESS?

My starting point is always that this is exactly what the word suggests—a negotiation. It's not a "Get everything my own way" exercise.

For a negotiation to be a success, there needs to be respect for the other party and their goals. You need to be prepared for compromise. A successful negotiation is where both parties get something of what they wanted, but not everything.

Sure, there will always be elements of a negotiation where either party is not willing to budge on certain matters, but generally there is always a way to find some middle ground.

I think again of how Nelson Mandela handled the negotiation of power transfer in the process of creating a democratic South Africa.

You think you have a tough business deal to negotiate? Well, try and negotiate the future of a country.

Mandela was a master negotiator in that he could make the other party feel at ease and part of the process, not simply a bystander. Of course, he had things he would not concede in the negotiation process. But he always treated people with respect and listened to their point.

I think it goes without saying that you never get personal in a negotiation. Stick to the facts of what you are negotiating, and then accept that there is always going to be plenty of that good old-fashioned give-and-take, and compromise.

When we do a deal to design a golf course, it's just as important for us to know what the developer wants out of the whole process as it is to make sure we get what we want. Know what you want, accept that you might not get 100 percent of that, and deal with respect.

If you want another real lesson in negotiation, look no further than my good friend Lee Trevino. Lee told me how one day he was cutting the grass at his home. It was a hot day, so he was wearing shorts and no shirt. A lady drove past and, not recognizing him, mistook him for being the gardener. She rolled down her window and asked, "How much do you charge for cutting lawn?" Lee says she was quite good-looking, so he said to her, "It's for free, but my deal is that I get to sleep with the lady of this house."

He says he'd never seen somebody speed off that fast.

11. I'M VERY RISK-AVERSE, BUT I KNOW MY BUSINESS NEEDS ME TO TAKE SOME RISKS NOW. WHAT ARE THE QUESTIONS I NEED TO ASK TO MAKE SURE I'M TAKING THE RIGHT RISKS AND NOT BEING RECKLESS?

Risk. You could write a book on this alone, especially when it comes to golf. Risk and reward is the common theme in every golfer's mind when he or she is taking on a shot. So approach it the same way by asking the first question, as you would do with that risky shot.

What do you want to achieve, and how important is it to you?

That will determine the level of risk that you are prepared to take.

In 1971, I took probably the biggest risk of my life. I stood in front of the most powerful man in South Africa. I had a question for him. It was not an easy question, and there was a part of me that knew I could be risking everything by asking it. But I had set my mind to it.

I had travelled to Cape Town to meet with Prime Minister BJ (Balthazar Johannes) Vorster at his offices. Vorster served as the prime minister of South Africa for 12 years from 1966 to 1978, and then as the state president from 1978 to 1979.

He had succeeded the architect of apartheid, Hendrik Verwoerd. He adhered to those self-same principles, albeit with a greater desire to improve South Africa's image and relations abroad, and more particularly with its neighboring African countries.

I was grateful that Vorster had decided to receive me. True, by 1971 I was very much a worldwide star. I had already completed the Grand Slam with my two Open Championship victories, a Masters, a PGA Championship, and a US Open.

But here I was, off the fairways and greens upon which I had always felt so comfortable, and within the halls of South African politics.

It did make it easier that I had played golf with Vorster on several occasions, and he shared my passion for the game.

My brother Ian always spoke of Vorster's great fondness for me. In fact, some of Vorster's closest advisors and political allies went so far as to refer to me as "Vossie's Seun" (Afrikaans for "Vossie's Boy"). We had a very good relationship notwithstanding my political position, and here I was about to risk it all.

I was ushered into Vorster's office, and after exchanging the usual pleasantries, he sat down behind his big oak desk and asked, "So Gary, what can I do for you?" There have been many defining moments in my golf career. But I can honestly say that this was one of the profound moments of my life. And that's when I asked him.

"I want to try to end apartheid in South African sport. Will you help me?"

He was silent for a few seconds. Then he leaned forward, rested his elbows on the desk, and glared at me from under those huge eyebrows he had. Still, he said nothing. At this point I thought he was going to have me thrown out of his office. He had recently banned the cricketer Basil D'Oliveira from competing in South Africa, and he'd also banned a Japanese jockey, Sueo Masuzawa, from competing in the country, as well as denying tennis legend Arthur Ashe a visa to visit South Africa.

Then he said, "What's your plan?"

I was flabbergasted. I told him I wanted to invite the African American golf professional Lee Elder to play golf in South Africa. Again, Vorster just stared at me. And then he said it.

"Go ahead."

So I did. I arranged that Elder play in the 1971 South African PGA Championship. Elder was the first black professional golfer to play in one of the three traditional "Major" tournaments in South African golf, the others being the South African Open and the South African Masters. It was also the first integrated sports event held in South Africa since apartheid became official government policy in 1948.

Bear in mind that Elder played in "racist South Africa" before he was even allowed to compete in big golf tournaments in his home country of the USA. It was only in 1975 that Elder became the first black professional to play in The Masters.

It was a step in the right direction toward bringing an end to apartheid.

Some may argue I was risking everything by getting involved in a political battle of which I shouldn't have been a part. But I felt the risk was worth it.

Knowing when to take a risk comes from experience.

When I was at the height of my playing career, I knew when to take a risk on a shot because I knew my game and capabilities.

It's the same in business. Know what you are capable of, and that will determine the level of risk you can take successfully.

On the golf course, if I had any doubt as to whether I could reach a green in two, I'd lay up because I knew I was going to be putting for a birdie. I limited my level of risk to the knowledge that I was a good wedge player and putter.

So it would have been reckless of me to try and take on the shot and hit it into the water.

I always approached it in the sense of knowing the strengths of my game and then visualizing my success based on those strengths.

I think a reckless risk is when you extend yourself beyond what you are capable of. A reckless risk is also taking on something you don't need to take on.

My favorite golf example of this is the 1999 Open Championship at Carnoustie and the case of Jean Van de Velde.

With a three-shot lead, Van de Velde hit a driver. Then he decided to go for the green. Why on earth did he make that decision? It was a risky shot and one he didn't need to take. Out of bounds on the left. Grandstands on the right. Water in the front. What? And all of this with a three-shot lead? C'mon. Ultimately it was a decision that cost him the championship.

When I had a two-shot lead playing the last hole there in 1968, I hit a 3 iron, a 4 iron, and then a 9 iron onto the green.

There was just no need to take a risk in that situation.

Take the risk, by all means. But then know very clearly what your strengths are. And your limits. I can't stress how important it is to know your limits when assessing risk. We all have limits, and to believe otherwise is foolish.

And when you commit to the risk, then commit wholeheartedly.

I've never regretted making a decision. That doesn't mean all my decisions have turned out fine. Some have not. But I've never regretted making a decision.

If you feel now is the time to take a risk in your business, and you've weighed up all the pros and cons, then go for it. Believe in your decision, and in yourself.

12. I'M THINKING OF A CAREER CHANGE. IT'S RADICALLY DIFFERENT FROM WHAT I'M DOING NOW. PEOPLE ARE TELLING ME I SHOULD STICK TO WHAT I KNOW. WHAT WOULD YOUR ADVICE BE?

It depends where you are in your life. If you're still young, you can afford to take a chance on venturing down a new path, but if you're a bit older, then it becomes more risky.

If you're older, I'd suggest you start slowly. When I wanted to indulge my passion for horses and saw myself getting into the thoroughbred business, I didn't just quit golf and throw myself into this new business. I started small by buying first one horse, then a few more, and slowly I built up this side of my business while I was still playing.

Now it has grown into something I can do full-time after my playing career.

I don't know what circumstances are pushing you to make this change, but approach it with patience.

There is merit in sticking with what you know. But then again, apart from riding horses from an early age, I knew nothing about breeding them. I had to learn. And this was maybe a good thing because it meant I couldn't just jump headlong into this new venture. I had to be patient and take it step by step.

But it's important to note that I did at least have some experience with horses. I think in your situation it's important to ascertain whether this new career path you are considering resonates in any way with your life experience. It's amazing how what we go through in life often comes in handy later. Never discount the value of experience. Going completely blind into something is not always the best approach.

13. I'VE BEEN IN A REALLY TOUGH TIME WITH MY BUSINESS, SPECIFICALLY DUE TO THE IMPACT OF THE GLOBAL ECONOMY FOR A FEW YEARS NOW. HOW DO I GET THAT FIGHT BACK IN ME TO TAKE ON THE CHALLENGES AND SEEK SOLUTIONS?

Life is a challenge. Accept it, and meet it head-on.

Life is like winning Majors—it's not easy. Winning Majors is far more challenging than winning your average tour event. And that's how it should be. It shouldn't be easy. The biggest challenges of your life are exactly that—the biggest. It's your final examination paper, and it's not supposed to be easy. If it were, then winning a Major wouldn't be associated with the word "great." It would simply be good.

Accept that you are facing a great challenge, and see in it the ability to bring out greatness in you.

I did this my whole career, and I've even brought this philosophy into my golf course design business.

If there is one course that really embodies a lot of who I am as a competitor, it's The Links at Fancourt in South Africa. That golf course is all about the challenge. Life is a challenge, and for me The Links reflects this.

When I was a young man, there was really nowhere in South Africa where I could prepare myself properly for the challenge of going over and playing the links courses in Britain. The first time I saw Carnoustie, I said to myself, *How do you play this golf course? It's just too tough.* It was just such a change of thinking for me. I played Carnoustie in a tremendous wind, and I thought, *What an amazing challenge this is. It's going to raise my game, no doubt about it.* So when I sat down to discuss the design of The Links, that's what I had in mind—to create a true links challenge similar to Carnoustie. I wanted a golf course where people could experience the difficulties of golf in Scotland, a course where they couldn't just get going and make birdie after birdie after birdie. Accepting adversity is part of a round of golf, and part of what makes a champion, not just making birdies.

I wanted to make golfers think. Today, they would play a hole downwind and tomorrow into the wind. Today, 164 yards would be a 9 iron and tomorrow it's a 3 iron. That's why I say, if you want to have an experience, you play The Links. If you want to have a playable round of golf where you can make lots of birdies, then there are other courses to do that on. If you look at a course like Carnoustie, it's harsh and most often cruel. It will take the slightest weakness in your game and tear it all to shreds. But whatever all the great golfers think of Carnoustie, one thing is clear—everybody respects it. And when I first went to play the Old Course at St. Andrews, I was a cocky little guy and they asked me what I thought about it. My reply was, "You know, they spoiled a good marsh." Now of course I know it's a masterpiece. It's the challenge. That is what I enjoyed the most throughout my career—the challenge.

And never forget your yesterdays. I believe you let your yesterdays build your tomorrows. That foundation you have built up over so many years is what is going to get you through this challenge. That's what helps you to refocus and adapt to a new challenge.

14. THE COMPANY I WORK FOR IS BUSY DOWNSIZING AND THERE IS THIS CULTURE OF FEAR IN THE OFFICE. EVERYBODY IS WORRIED ABOUT THEIR JOB SECURITY. HOW DO I NOT SUCCUMB TO THIS FEAR AND PROVE I'M STILL A VALUABLE ASSET?

Fear is crippling.

You're obviously right to feel an element of fear. Nobody wants to be at risk of losing their job, but you cannot prove what a valuable asset you are if you're working from a base of fear.

Fear makes you defensive. You need to have the strength to play your own game, so to speak. No matter what. You need to shift the focus away from the fear and back to your game plan. And no matter what is going on around you or what others are doing, you need to stick to your game plan.

The great golfers like Jack Nicklaus and Ben Hogan, when they were playing their best, had a tremendous calm about them.

It's so easy to get sidetracked from what you have set out to do. There are so many factors pulling our minds in different directions every single moment of every day. It can be the challenges of juggling a family with your career aspirations. It can be work colleagues feeding you negative thoughts. It can even be your boss, whose own indecision influences your strategy on a particular project, or whose negative words are now influencing the way you feel about your future in the company.

But trust yourself. That's when the best of you will come out. That's not to say the circumstances around you will improve or be any less daunting.

Golf is the one game where you can go from one day of doing everything right to another of not knowing why everything is going wrong.

The shot I hit on the par-five 14th hole during the final round of the 1968 Open at Carnoustie filled me with fear at the time. I remember standing at my drive and just wrestling with the decision as to whether to go for the green with my second shot and try and carry the fearsome Spectacles bunkers, or to play safe.

Nicklaus had just hit a brilliant recovery shot and was pushing hard to win the tournament. He wasn't the only one. I knew that there were a few players just ready to pounce at the slightest mistake I made.

But I calmed myself down.

I reached for a 3 wood. I went on to hit one of the finest shots of my career. The ball finished 14 inches from the hole, and I holed the eagle putt for a two-shot lead. That gave me the cushion I need to go on and win.

When I hit that shot, everything around me had fear written all over it. There was the fear that I was making the wrong decision. The fear that I might hit a bad shot and lose the championship. The fear posed by the threat of the other players around me. The fear of seeing that several other players were starting to succumb to the difficult course and were dropping shots around me.

In your situation, you know a similar fear. The fear of your colleagues being laid off, and when is it going to be your turn? The fear of whether the company you work for even has a future. The fear of where you will find another job. The fear of how you will pay your bills or support your family.

You need to just calm yourself down, decide on your plan, and get back to doing what made you an asset for the company in the first place.

Much like that shot at Carnoustie, once you've decided on your game plan, keep your head down, commit, and follow through with everything you have.

15. I'VE MADE A FEW WRONG CALLS IN MY BUSINESS OF LATE, AND IT'S AFFECTED MY CONFIDENCE AND ABILITY TO MAKE EFFECTIVE DECISIONS. HOW DID YOU BOUNCE BACK FROM SOME BAD BUSINESS DECISIONS?

By accepting that I'm human.

Mistakes are a fact of life. We all make them.

You may now be on what golfers call "the bogey train." That's when a golfer just starts making bogeys and can't stop. It erodes his confidence and makes even a 3-foot putt that he's holed hundreds of times over the years seem like a monster.

So accept that you're having a bad run, and that you're not the first or the last.

Then get back to basics.

Whenever I found I was starting to lose it out on the golf course, I'd just try and center myself again mentally.

So start by just getting a bit of calm back into your mind. Then take a few steps back.

It's perfectly fine to take a few steps back to be able to move forward. We tend to see this as a weakness or a failure. But taking a few steps back to correct your mistakes, or at least to properly analyze why you're making them, is often vital and can lead to even greater success than just blindly pushing forward with no clear idea of why.

And if you've made a bad decision and it's cost you, accept it as such.

It's like a bad round of golf. You can do nothing to change it. Sometimes you've just got to get through it, chalk it up to experience, and move on.

But move on positively. Forget about it and don't dwell on it. There is a great saying, "When you lose, don't lose the lesson."

It's the dwelling on our mistakes that affects our confidence the most. We start to get personal about the mistake and see it in the context of our shortcomings rather than for what it was: just a bad decision.

It has nothing to do with who you are in terms of defining you for the rest of your life. It is just a question of a decision you made at that particular time.

So don't let these bad decisions start a process where you question yourself and your abilities. Do not let a bad decision define you. We all make bad decisions, just like as golfers we all hit poor putts. I've hit millions of putts in my life. Over the majority of those putts, I can guarantee you that I've walked around them, looked at the line and considered the pace from every angle, asked my caddie for his opinion, and then decided exactly how I am going to hit this putt to get the best result—the ball in the hole.

But you know what, there have been countless times where I've done all of this, and the ball didn't end up in the hole. Did I start to question my putting skills? No, because there were a lot of other times where the ball did end up in the hole. Did I move on to the next hole thinking I couldn't putt? No. I moved on to the next hole and went about the same process, determined to make that next putt.

I also know that the way you start making long putts again is by practicing short ones and getting used to the feeling you once knew so well—that of a putt dropping into the bottom of the hole.

I can guarantee you that you are not going to make every putt you put all of your effort into on the golf course. Just as I can guarantee that you are not going to get every decision right, no matter how much effort you have put into the making of that decision.

But you know what? You can miss a putt on the 17th green and still win the tournament by making another putt on the 18th.

16. IF YOU WERE HIRING A CEO FOR YOUR BUSINESS, WHAT QUALITIES WOULD YOU LOOK FOR?

I couldn't ask for a better CEO of Black Knight International than my son Marc, because he has a shared vision of what we both want to achieve.

I think that is vital. You need to be on the same page.

You cannot have a caddie that doesn't believe in your ability, and similarly you need a CEO who shares what you want to do with your company.

Anybody can get the best business degree in the world, but it doesn't mean they're best suited to lead your particular business.

Marc understands me better than almost anybody does. He knows what drives me and is able to translate this into the sound business decisions he makes.

It's also enabled him to take us into new areas and create great opportunities for our business.

I think respect is also key. A CEO must have respect for the company he or she works for and the people who help to make that company successful.

Humility is another great quality in a CEO. Some of the greatest business leaders I have been around have been incredibly humble men and women. They have never taken their success for granted. In my own career, I always treated my talent as something that was on loan to me, that I was a custodian of and that I needed to treat with respect. I believe the CEO who takes a similar view of the leadership gift he or she has been given is the CEO I want to do business with.

This also extends to having the same work ethic that I have.

My day begins at 5 a.m., and I put 100 percent into everything I do that day, whether it be meeting sponsors, exercising, playing golf, or planting trees on my farm.

Arnold Palmer once said of me, "Gary worked as hard as anyone I've ever known—in golf or anything else."

If my brother Ian taught me to never give up and believe in myself, then it was my father who taught me how to work hard. My dad did an excellent job of showing me how much a man can achieve if he just knuckles down to the hard work.

I remember him inviting me to visit him at work on the mine. I waited at the mine entrance until he came up with the skip. I'll never forget the sight of him when he stepped out—this huge man with a big hat on, and sopping wet right down to his boots. We went into this locker room. The walls were lined with these steel lockers, and there was a drain in the middle of the floor. My dad took off his boots and poured the water in them into this drain.

I asked him, "Where'd you get all that water from?" and he said, "No, that's sweat."

He went down into that mine for 30 years and worked his tail off. He started when he was 15 because his father died, and he was the oldest, so he had to go and make a living. The only place that would take a 15-year-old boy was a mine. Seeing him work as hard as he did inspired me to do the same.

And I want a CEO who shares that work ethic, that philosophy, and that passion.

17. SOMETIMES I FEEL LIKE ALL THE FUN HAS GONE OUT OF MY WORK AND EVERYTHING HAS JUST BECOME SO SERIOUS. I FEEL LIKE I'VE LOST THE PASSION FOR WHAT I DO. HOW DO I GET THAT BACK?

I know a very intelligent woman who says there is a reason they call work labor—because it's not meant to be fun.

I always have a good laugh at that, because just saying it reminds me to check myself and get that fun back into my work when I feel like it's flagging a bit.

You know what? You've got to make the fun in your work. You've got to create the passion. Never lose sight that work is never as serious as you think it is.

I remember one year I was playing in the World Series in Akron, Ohio. I climbed in my courtesy car, and we left for the golf course one morning. We hit a massive traffic jam. I could see the course, but we just weren't moving. I knew I wasn't going to make my tee-off time. I started panicking. I could've sat there and just panicked, and would definitely have missed my tee-off time.

But then I saw this hippie on a motorbike. I jumped out of the car and stopped him, and I said, "I'll give you $50 if you give me a lift to that golf course." He agreed. So there I was, wearing these white pants and with my golf clubs on my back, sitting on the back of a motorbike and speeding to the course. We drove straight through the security, so they were chasing us to the clubhouse, as well. But I made the tee off. The press got a hold of the story, and the next day the headline read: *Hell's Angel gets Player to the tee on time.*

Even in the most serious moments, you can find a way to have fun.

One time I was playing an exhibition match against Billy Casper at Kyalami Golf Club in South Africa. On one hole, I hit a big hook. And would you believe it, out of 7,000 people there, I managed to hit my mother-in-law on the knee. When I got to her she said, "Yes, I know you were aiming for me." I replied, "Mom, if I was aiming at you I would've hit you on the head."

Even when it came to competing against my rivals like Jack Nicklaus and Arnold Palmer, I tried never to lose my sense of humor.

I was particularly fond of pulling practical jokes on them.

On one trip, we went to Zambia and we travelled through this thick bush at night. The locals were telling us about all these Gaboon Viper snakes and how deadly they were. Of course, we were a little concerned about that.

We checked into our hotel. Mark McCormack and Arnold were in a room together on the third floor. Later that night, with everybody still thinking about those Gaboon Vipers, I climbed out of our window and walked along the balcony, which was only a few feet wide. Bear in mind that I'm very afraid of heights, but I managed to squeeze along that balcony all the way to Mark and Arnold's room. Then I pressed my face right up against their window and slapped my hands on it. Mark looked up, saw this apparition, and got such a fright he screamed, "Arnold!" Arnold came running out of the next room with a golf club, ready to hit the first thing he saw. I began laughing like hell but had to hang on, as well. I shouted to them, "Open the bloody window before I fall to my death." They were kind enough to let me in after that.

Another time, Arnold, Jack, and myself shared a hotel suite in Canada. Arnold was on the phone talking to his wife. I then took this big champagne bottle, shook it up real good, and squirted it all over him. He said, "Winnie, I've got to go. Gary's picking a fight with me." He put the phone down, grabbed this ice bucket, and threw the water at me. But I ducked, and it went all over the curtains. Then I squirted Jack, as well, and Arnold hit him with the ice water. So Jack took the nearest thing to him, which was this plate full of little cakes, and started throwing those at us. We made an almighty mess of things.

The next day, we went and saw the manager and expressed our regret at what we'd done. "We made a bit of a mess of your suite," we told him, all of us feeling quite ashamed. We told him to please have it redone and send us the bill. But he was a keen golfer and told us not to worry about it.

Jack and I had a very intense rivalry, but it never stopped us from having a bit of fun on the golf course. During the 1965 Australian Open, for example, which took place at Kooyanga Golf Club, I shot 62 and Jack opened with a 66. We were staying in the same hotel. He saw me later and said, "How can I shoot 66 and

be four behind you? Tomorrow I'm going to catch you, you little bugger."

The next day I shot 70 and Jack shot 63. He moved to 129 and I was at 132. So after being four in front, now I'm three behind. We met up at the hotel, and I said, "How can I have an average of 66 and still be three shots behind you? Tomorrow I'm going to get your big, fat ass."

The next day, I was 10 under through 10 holes. I missed a 3-footer on the ninth for a 27. But I eagled the 10th hole. After that 10th hole, Jack's caddie comes running over to me and says, "Jack wants to know how you're doing today?"

"Tell him I'm 10 under," I said.

"No, not for the tournament, for your round," the caddie replied.

"That is for my round." I remember the caddie going back to tell Jack, and seeing him look across the other fairway at me and smile, then mouthing, "You bloody liar."

I shot 62 to win with a total of 264, which is still an Australian Open tournament record.

Never lose your sense of humor in your work.

18. THE INDUSTRY I WORK IN IS VERY COMPETITIVE AND QUITE CUTTHROAT. IT FEELS LIKE MY COLLEAGUES WILL DO ANYTHING JUST TO GET AHEAD. I'M JUST AS DRIVEN, BUT I DON'T WANT TO BECOME SOMEBODY I'M NOT. HOW DO YOU MAINTAIN A BALANCE IN BEING COMPETITIVE?

You can be competitive without losing perspective in the process.

That's why I love the game of golf so much. In our game, you do your best to win and beat your opponent, but never at the expense of comprising the values of our game.

Look at the Ryder Cup. Two continents select their best golfers and then they do their best to beat each other. They give everything. I think there are few competitions in sports that can match the intensity and passion of the Ryder Cup.

But when that intensity goes too far, then golf is self-correcting. We have had occasions in the Ryder Cup where as a collective we have all agreed that this is not the spirit in which this competition should be played. Yes, we all want to win. Yes, we all want to play the best and beat our opponents. But golf is pretty unique in the sense that we have the code of wanting to do so in the right way.

Isn't it amazing that in golf, those moments when two competitors have shown great sportsmanship have gone down in our sport's history as equally as significant as some of the greatest triumphs on the course?

That's also what you want to achieve in business. You want to be known as a fierce competitor who always does his or her best to achieve a win, but never at the expense of what we know is socially and morally acceptable.

I do not believe in a win-at-all-costs mentality, and nobody will ever convince me of its merits. Frankly, when we aspire to win at all costs, we lose on so many other fronts.

There is nothing wrong with being competitive. It's how the world and humanity moves forward. Where people get it wrong is when their competitive nature makes them lose respect for those around them.

Among Arnold Palmer, Jack Nicklaus, and myself, I don't think you could've found a more competitive bunch on the tour. We were competing for Majors, and believe me, every time we stepped onto the tee we wanted to beat the hell out of one another. Heck, we wanted to beat one another playing cards.

Even when I made my debut as an honorary starter at The Masters with Arnold and Jack a few years ago, you could bet I wanted to hit it farther than both of them.

But we respected one another too much to let our competitiveness ever affect our friendship. We travelled together, stayed in one another's homes, and remained friends throughout our careers. Even our wives were great friends. And because of our respect for one another, we could be three of the most dominant players in the history of the game without ever losing our friendship.

Be competitive. Chase your margins. Work for greater profits. But never ever let it come at the expense of your respect for your fellow businessman. Retain that respect for the person you're competing against, and that will ensure you retain perspective and balance in the heat of competition.

If your opponent is losing his respect for you and you somehow feel you've let him get the better of you because he was either more ruthless or willing to do something you wouldn't, then be happy within yourself that you haven't compromised your standards or the kind of competitor you want to be.

You can win ugly, but it will then always be remembered as an ugly victory.

Remember, Jack Nicklaus is lauded even more for his many second-place finishes and how gracious he was in defeat than he is for his 18 Major victories.

CONCLUSION

Wisdom.

It's something we all seek.

But wisdom is not some gift you suddenly receive. It is the culmination of years and years of experience. It comes to you in the most amazing ways and from all of the many experiences you have had in life—good and bad.

I was never a great artist. When my school art teacher, Mr. Mills, once said to us, "There is beauty in curvature," I did not think too much of it at the time. After all, I reasoned, what is a professional golfer going to do with that information?

Years later, I would smile to myself as I worked on my golf swing—focusing on that smooth arc—and in my mind I could hear Mr. Mills's words again. As a professional golfer, I could indeed appreciate the beauty he spoke of.

It was this same Mr. Mills who stood at my desk one day and asked me, "Gary, what do you want to do with your life?"

"I want to be a champion golfer," I told him.

"Well, then you'd better learn to sign your name clearly because you can't read half the signatures of these bloody athletes."

I am proud to say that to this day you know when Gary Player has signed something for you, because you can read it clearly.

Later on in life, I learned that you grow more through your failures than your successes. I also learned that I'm not much of a car man. After I won the Kentucky Derby Open in 1958, a fellow professional said to me, "Take my Cadillac and drive it to the next tournament. I'll meet you there."

It seemed like a great idea. I mean, who wouldn't enjoy a ride in a Cadillac? I was so excited. So I immediately got on the road. Suddenly, the wipers started going for no reason, and I couldn't get them to stop. I stopped the car, took the shoelaces out of my shoes, and tied those wipers down. Then a few miles farther, the bonnet jumped up for no reason. Again I stopped, and this time I took my belt off and used that to tie it down. A few more miles down the road, the car broke down. A policeman pulled me over, thinking I was drunk. I said to him, "Officer, I'm not drunk. But I think this Cadillac is trying to kill me." When I finally got to the next tournament, I took the keys to the gentleman and said, "Thanks, but you can have your Cadillac."

My grandchildren have also taught me so much, most importantly that I'm still the best cowboy on the block when it comes to a game of Cowboys and Indians.

When I celebrated my 80th birthday, I was privileged to have so many friends from all around the world join me at a wonderful party we enjoyed at the Sun City Resort in South Africa.

It was a magnificent evening. As I went around the room chatting with everybody and shaking hands, I was again astounded by how many influential people—leaders, business giants, sports stars, celebrities, and people from many other walks of life—were there.

I have learned so much from so many of them.

Some people in my life have spent a great deal of time sharing with me their life lessons. From others, such as the great Ben Hogan, I learned more about golf from just watching him than I did from anything he ever said. And he said very little.

I am always willing to learn. I believe in lifelong learning, and I hope you'll take this as the greatest lesson from this book and my life.

I believe wisdom is learned. I have never been ashamed to say I don't know something. But I would be ashamed if I didn't at least know somebody I could ask for an answer. Be sure to keep learning and keep growing as a human being.

I hope this book has helped you and given you some insight into how I've made decisions throughout my life and how this had led to my success, not just in golf and business, but in life in general. And I hope it helps you to live the life you choose and to live it well.